Launch Yourself
creating a new normal one intention at a time

David Trotter

Copyright © 2010 by David Trotter

All rights reserved.
No part of this publication may be reproduced or transmitted
in any form or by any means, electronic or mechanical, including photocopy,
recording or any other information storage and retrieval system,
without prior permission in writing from the publisher.

Published in the United States by Nurmal Resources.

Library of Congress Control Number: 2010913890

ISBN-13 9781935798057
ISBN-10 1935798057

Printed in the United States of America

Design and layout by 8TRACKstudios
www.8TRACKstudios.com

Author photo by Shauntelle Sposto

To Randy Powell

Thank you for shining a light
in the dark spaces and
walking with me as I
re-launched my life.

Launch Yourself Workbook
ISBN - 9781935798064

The accompanying workbook is an excellent tool
for individuals and small group participants to
process Launch Yourself principles
in their own lives.

Contents
creating a new normal

Preface	6
Getting The Life You've Always Wanted	9
01. I Got Stuck With This Life…Can We Trade?	11
02. Remember When…	23
03. What if?	33
The Process of Intention	45
04. Who Am I?	47
05. What Do I Want?	59
06. What Truths Will Keep Me Focused?	71
07. How Will I Take Action?	83
08. Who Will Walk With Me?	93
The Seven Spheres of Transformation	107
09. Life Passions	109
10. Romance	121
11. Community	135
12. Money and Possessions	149
13. Creativity and Play	163
14. Physical Well-being	177
15. Spirituality	189
16. Head Up, Shoulders Back, One Step Forward	203
Acknowledgements	217

Preface
my heart for you

In the beginning of 2008, I just couldn't take it anymore. I was sick of my marriage and burned out on my job. I felt completely stuck with my life, and I had no clue how to get out of the mess I created for myself. I wanted out.

From a cursory look at my life, you would have never known.

I had been married 14 years, and we had two beautiful children. My wife was a kindergarten teacher who was both attractive and a saint in the eyes of others. I had a high-profile job as the founder and leader of a growing non-profit. No debt other than a mortgage and one car payment. Life was good…or so it looked from the outside.

On the inside, I was dying. I lacked the freedom and peace I longed for in my life. Even though my wife was amazing, I didn't see her as a partner in the truest sense of the word. I was constantly tired and run down from working 70-80 hours a week, and I had few close friends to speak of.

I was dying a slow death.

Fed up with everything, I finally decided on a re-launch, but things didn't turn out exactly as planned. Although I radically changed the direction of my life with a few decisions, this led to a chain of events ultimately landing me in a psych hospital for three dark days.

At my lowest point, I questioned if I wanted to press on in this life. Somehow, I continued to believe that I could truly have the life I longed for, but I had no clue how to find it. The only thing I could do was ask questions…the same questions…over and over and over again. These five questions seemed to keep emerging every time I'd come up against a challenge or opportunity.

These questions, what I now call The Process of Intention, led me out of the darkest season of my soul toward the new life I hoped would finally emerge.

Two and a half years later, I have a new normal.

> I have more freedom in my life than ever before…
> and I'm not overwhelmed with work.
>
> I'm developing the marriage I've always wanted…
> but it still requires effort.
>
> I love my children more than ever…
> but my patience is ever-growing.
>
> I have many new friendships now…
> which used to be few and far between.

I have a new normal, because I was willing to make some intentional decisions to find the life I truly wanted. Are you living the life you truly want? If not, I invite you to start asking intentional questions and experiencing the transformation that's available to all of us. A new normal awaits you.

David Trotter
Lakewood, California
August 2010

Getting The Life You've Always Wanted

section 1

You have one life to live.
The question is...how will you invest it?

If you live a full life, you'll exist in your 'earth suit' for 70, 80, or maybe even 90 years. In my case, my intention is to live until I'm 100 years old...and enjoy every moment including my final breath.

You do realize that your *intentions* have everything to do with the type of life you experience, don't you? If you intend to live a rich, meaningful life with intimate relationships and creative expression, that's the kind of life you'll live. On the other hand, if you intend to live a life of working 9 to 5 and waiting for the weekend to roll around, you can definitely experience that instead.

It's your choice.

You have the power to create intentions that will change the course of your life.

My guess is that you've come to some sort of realization recently causing you to desire something different in this life. Perhaps, you've been longing to live out your passions or begin a new romantic relationship or develop a greater degree of physical health. Whatever reason provoked you to pick up this book, your intentions will determine whether you take action to re-launch your life or not.

Write Your Own Permission Slip
Remember in elementary school the fear of forgetting your permission slip for the biggest field trip of the year? My teacher (and probably yours) threatened the entire class with the dreaded consequence of being left behind.

No one wanted to be *the only kid left behind*. The fear of having to sit in on another class felt so overwhelming that every one of us would find a way to get the single-most important piece of paper back into our teacher's hands…*with* our parent's signature emblazoned upon it.

The idea of 'permission' has been so ingrained in most of our minds (for good reason at an early age) that many of us are still looking for permission as adults.

Instead of feeling the freedom to pursue what's in our hearts, we're waiting around for someone to give us permission to re-launch our lives. Ironically, they (whoever 'they' is) don't even know we're waiting for them to say something…nor would they think we needed their permission to begin with. Oftentimes, the need for permission is so nebulous that no one can give us the thumbs up other than ourselves.

What do you feel like you need permission to do? What exactly is it? Feel free to write your own permission slip, and let's experience a life launch together!

I Got Stuck With This Life... Can We Trade?
chapter 01

As my head hit the pillow, it was starting to dawn on me.
I was stuck...stuck in a life I hadn't set out to create.

It was one of those unedited moments of life where all the background noise of the day had faded away. The kids were tucked into bed, and my wife was sound asleep from helping 25 first graders sit relatively still and learn all they can in between recesses. The flickering TV was finally off, and the laptop that was an extension of my own hands was stowed under the side of the bed...just in case I needed it in the middle of the night.

My brain was winding down from its incessant processing as I tried to figure out how to continually fund the non-profit I founded. I was turning down the flow of worry that usually opened its valves full-blast that time of night...especially about management issues surrounding my staff.

That's when it surfaces, doesn't it?

That's when the deepest, lingering feelings start to escape the locked recesses of our heart where we try to hide them from the world around us…and even from ourselves.

If I actually feel what's going on down there, I may have to come to grips with what those emotions are telling me. I might actually have to do something about the feelings of boredom or dissatisfaction or hopelessness.

Despite my best efforts to bury them…my dissatisfactions with life started trickling to the surface one by one.

I was stuck in my career – sick and tired of financial and management issues. I was bored in my marriage – more like roommates than anything else. I was overwhelmed by my kids – driving me nuts constantly. I was disappointed in my friendships – which barely even existed. I was depressed about my weight – heavier than I had ever been. And, I was tired of not having enough money – longing for more freedom.

That pretty much wrapped up my entire life. I was stuck in a long rut, and I didn't know how to get out.

If you came to me with this same scenario asking for advice, I would have been able to lay out a strategic, 10 step plan to turn your life around. In fact, that was somewhat of my job. I was in the business of helping people make significant changes in their lives.

Ironically, I was the one who was stuck, and all I could think about was trading my life for a new one.

Remember in elementary school when your mom packed that pimento cheese sandwich in your lunch? Or, maybe it was liverwurst…or Spam…or whatever made you gag. You were stuck with it, weren't you?

That is…unless you were able to talk the weird kid who actually liked that crap into trading with you.

That's what I wanted to do. I was dying to trade my life for something else…something adventurous and romantic and fun.

Frankly, I didn't want to do the hard work of making intentional choices in order to climb my way out of the ditch I had dug over the course of 14 years of marriage. I didn't want to re-think my life's calling after investing 10 years of hard work into building a specific approach to my non-profit leadership.

Pretty soon I found myself sitting in a therapist's office spilling my guts. I went on and on about all the woes of my life and how completely dissatisfied I was.

"David, do you think there's a possibility that your marriage could be saved?" the therapist asked with an air of optimism.

After hearing all his great insight and ideas, I finally let this guy have it…there was no way he was going to talk me into loving the life I had. I was done!

"Sure, my marriage could be saved…if I actually wanted claw my way out of a hole the size of the Grand Canyon! I'd rather just blow it all up and start over."

So, that's what I did.

I left my wife for her best friend, and we moved in together. I resigned from the non-profit I founded, and I started living off $3,000 in cash and a credit card with a $32,000 limit.

Let's just say…*I wasn't stuck anymore!* I launched myself in a completely different direction. I was intentionally creating a new life, but it didn't exactly turn out the way I had hoped.

My wife's best friend left me after six weeks, and she moved back in with her husband and four kids. After throwing away a 14-year marriage and a 10-year career, I was rendered completely non-functional, and I checked myself into a hospital for three days to get some desperately needed help. After I got out, I moved 30 minutes away from my family to be near friends, and I battled suicide for a couple of weeks…that is, until I apologized to my wife and set the trajectory of my heart back toward her.

What transpired over the next two years was a windy road that led to reconciliation with my wife and kids, the development new friendships, the start of several businesses, and ultimately…the re-launching of my life.

Do You Have the Life You've Always Wanted?
Thankfully, most of us don't feel *that* bad about life…nor do we do something that drastic to find the life we've always wanted. Yet, recent studies show that over 10% of the American population (that's more than 27 million people) are taking anti-depressants on a daily basis.

What does that tell you?

It tells me that we're a culture in acute need of feeling better about our lives. We want meaning and purpose out of our days. We long for intimate relationships with our lovers and our friends. We desire a life that's creative and enjoyable…yet something is preventing us from experiencing it.

Unfortunately, many of us are simply medicating ourselves, not just with anti-depressants, but with alcohol, drugs, affairs, overspending, and any other 'hit' that will take off the edge of meaninglessness in our lives.

The truth is that life dissatisfaction is the result of living an unintentional life.

Rather than remaining stuck in an existence you never wanted, I am inviting you to capture a vision to re-launch yourself with a trajectory toward a rich and meaningful life.

To get started, I want to challenge you to think about your current situation. What's not going as well as you'd like it to?

Most of us go to the extremes when we encounter areas of dissatisfaction. Some of us worry, blame, and complain about it every chance we get. Others of us just shove that dissatisfaction deeper and deeper into our hearts so that we won't have to actually deal with it.

I want you to get honest about what's really going on in your life...right now.

To help you think through the satisfaction level, let's look at what I call "The Seven Spheres of Transformation"...

1. Life Passions

Everyone has 'life passions' that are waiting to be discovered. These are divinely imprinted interests that are without explanation. Although someone in our lives may have introduced us to them early on, something stuck in a way that other things didn't. This may be a passion for medicine, construction, baseball, or art. It could be a zeal for cooking, interior design, or plants. I don't know what it is for you, but you'll need to discover it in order to have the life you've always wanted.

It's not a matter of whether you were given a life passion or not. The question is...have you discovered what you're passionate about? Once you've made that discovery, the next step is to live it out in a way that leaves a mark on this great world where we spend a few short years.

You may have heard it said this way, "Find something you love so much that you'd be willing to do it for free...then find someone to pay you to do it." Are you living that kind of life? Or, does it seem ludicrous that it's actually a possibility?

2. Romance

Although there are some individuals who have no interest in a romantic relationship (perhaps because of negative experiences or their life stage), I find that most people long to develop an intimacy with someone who will love them authentically. We were created with a desire to love and be loved, and sexuality is a major part of that.

If you're single, are you confident in who you are? Are you comfortable with loving yourself so that you're available to love someone else? If you're married, are you passionate about your spouse? Are they truly your partner in life or simply a roommate? Or, an inmate? Be honest with yourself…do you have the romance your truly want in your life?

3. Community

A healthy individual usually has 1-3 very intimate friends, a circle of 10-20 ongoing friendships, 20-75 meaningful connections, and an unlimited number of acquaintances. If a person is significantly lacking in any of these areas, most likely there is a missing sense of community that can leave one feeling empty and disconnected.

Mutually beneficial friendships at different levels of intimacy create a deep sense of satisfaction in life. There's nothing like experiencing the comfort of being with others who know you and embrace you…just for being you.

Unfortunately, so many of our relationships in school and the workplace are based on *performance*. "If you perform the way I want you to, then we can continue the relationship as it is. If not, things will change." True friendship begins to move beyond a need to *perform* for other people to a more authentic connection.

Do you have friendships that are meaningful to you? Do you have a few people that would walk with you through life…no matter what?

4. Money and Possessions

Money is merely a tool to provide the resources you need to sustain your life. The question quickly becomes...how much is actually enough? Our culture tells us that we can never have enough... but many of us go into deep debt trying to accumulate *bigger and better stuff*.

The bigger house, the nicer car, the fancier clothes, and the latest and greatest gadgets are calling your name constantly. They call out to you through advertisements and through the testimony of others telling you how much you need whatever it is that you don't have.

How does your view of money impact the way you spend your time, the job you have, and the possessions you obtain? Are you satisfied with the income you generate? Does it cover your necessities? Or, do you always feel like you're coming up short? What role does generosity play in your lifestyle?

5. Creativity and Play

As a kid, we're given the freedom to be creative and play almost all day long – every day. That is...until we go to kindergarten. Then, we're taught how to play nice with others and be creative within the boundaries of a teacher. And, in most schools, creativity is encouraged just a little bit less and less until we finally make it to college. In this time of preparation for the 'real world', we're taught facts, statistics, and techniques that are tried and true. Until finally we make it out into the workforce...where creativity is usually sucked out of us completely.

That may not be the case for you, but for millions of Americans, the day to day grind of a job is just that...a grind. There isn't much room for creativity or playfulness. We have a job to do, and the company's future is determined by how effective and efficient we become.

Ironically, it's creativity and playfulness that rejuvenate the soul and stimulate the mind to be even more effective. Are you making room for the creative in your life? Or, has someone squeezed it out of you in hopes of turning you into a drone that just gets the job done?

6. Physical Well-being

Most of us would like to believe we can live a sedentary lifestyle and eat whatever we want and still feel satisfied about ourselves. What we fail to embrace is the fact that our physical health and well-being are inextricably tied to our mental, emotional, and spiritual experiences in life. We are interconnected beings with physical bodies in need of care and nurturing.

What level of intentionality do you have when it comes to providing your body with nutrition that will serve as fuel – not just satisfying your cravings? Are you finding that your body is cooperating with your mind, or do you feel constrained and limited? Do you feel energized and full of life, or are you struggling to get going? Are their health issues that you've been unwilling to face up until this point? Get gut-level honest about your health. Are you satisfied with the current state of your physical well-being?

7. Spirituality

If you're one of those few people who doesn't believe in a Higher Power or God or Allah or whatever name you give He/She/It, feel free to skip this section. But...for the rest of us, spirituality is a crucial component to experiencing a rich and meaningful life whether we realize it or not.

For the sake of this book, let's call this Being...God. If God created the heavens and the earth and you and me (somehow), perhaps God has a plan for our lives...not a secret plan to destroy us, but to give us a rich, meaningful life. If God created us, there is a sense that this Creator may know what's best for the creation. Maybe, God knows how we were designed to live.

I have to show my hand a bit. From my perspective, I believe that I was designed to love God and the people around me...to follow in God's footsteps by creating amazing things...and to consider everything around me as sacred. I have an incredible well of Wisdom, Strength, and Grace to draw upon. I want to eliminate any division between those things that are spiritual and non-spiritual in my life. All of life is spiritual in my eyes, and I'm seeking to live an integrated life.

To what degree is spirituality a meaningful part of your experience here on this earth? Do you believe there is a greater depth of experience you have yet to journey through?

A few years ago when I did this quick inventory, I came up feeling pretty empty. I looked at the dashboard of my life, and I was running in the red when it came to RPMs – working 70 to 80 hours a week. I glanced over at the fuel gauge, and it was in the red as well…and on top of that, the check engine light had been glowing in my face for quite some time.

I was done… my engine was burning up!

Perhaps you have been caught in a rut of drivenness and success like I was. On the other hand, maybe you find yourself with little drive at all. Maybe you find yourself in the rut of mere existence with hardly any meaningful reason to live other than waiting for carefree weekends to roll around.

Whatever perspective you're coming from, you are not alone.

Frankly, walking through these seven spheres of your life is meant to make you sick to your stomach. If you're feeling completely dissatisfied, I'm glad. I've earned myself an A+. The truth is that you were just as dissatisfied before you picked up this book, but you've probably been burying it as deep as possible…hoping it would just biodegrade in your soul. Unfortunately, it doesn't…and it won't. The dissatisfaction swirls around in our hearts until it finally starts to seep out of our lives.

For me, it leaked out by micro-managing my staff, worrying constantly about things out of my control, over-working to try to feel *in* control, and ultimately developing an interest in a woman other than my wife.

Finally, I just couldn't take it anymore, and I pushed the red detonation button. I blew it all up and left the shrapnel behind for a new life. Although my original plans didn't work out so well, I did end up creating the life I've always wanted.

In the midst of my leave-my-wife-for-her-best-friend adventure, my therapist commented, "I have to say how proud I am of you for what you're doing. You've intentionally sought out intimate romance, a new way to live out your passions, and an adventurous life….but I can't affirm *how* you've chosen to do it. You've made a complete mess in the process!"

He was right.

I made some very intentional decisions that were utterly reckless and irresponsible, and the shrapnel from my life flew in every direction. It hit my wife and kids the hardest. They were completely devastated by my decisions, and so were countless others.

As I was living all alone in an apartment 30 minutes away from my family, I had some difficult decisions to make. Would I give up, crawl into a hole, and beg God to take my life (or just do it myself)? Would I sign up for online dating and find a new, adventurous woman? Would I start over-working again – trying to lift myself up out of the pit of my own despair? Or, would I seek health and wholeness trusting that my future was bright even though I couldn't see evidence of it quite yet?

Believe me when I tell you…it wasn't an easy decision.

Thankfully, there were a few friends that re-surfaced when everyone else stayed away from my mess. They were willing to walk with me through the process of re-launching my life.

Over the course of two years, I discovered that *a life launch is the process of creating the life I've always wanted – one intention at a time*.

It's not about developing a master plan and living it out perfectly or all the time. We all know those don't work, and we end up more discouraged than ever!

It's about knowing who you've been created to be. It is the process of discovering what you really want out of life, embracing truths that will keep you focused, and taking intentional, practical steps toward the mental picture of your preferable future. And, it's about walking with other 'life launchers' along the way...people who are willing to journey with you through the ups and downs of life.

After hitting rock bottom, I made the courageous decision to pick up all the pieces and launch my life in a new direction...a path that would cause me to ask the same questions over and over ensuring that I was making the intentional decisions that would lead to my preferred life and the new normal I longed for.

- Who am I?
- What do I want?
- What truths will keep me focused?
- How will I take action?
- Who will walk with me?

By continually reflecting on the answers to these empowering questions, I was intentional about my own health along with the restoration of my relationship with my wife and kids...and I was miraculously welcomed back into our family's home six months after I abruptly left.

I have a new life and a new normal now.

It's not the life I thought I would have when I left on that dark day...it's even better! I have set my intentions toward a healthy, enjoyable, and adventurous life where I'm experiencing ongoing growth in all of The Seven Spheres of Transformation.

A life launch isn't a one-time experience...it's about a 'one-intention-at-a-time' experience. It's about living so intentionally that you're experiencing more of the life you've always wanted each and every day.

Remember When...
chapter 02

I lived most of my life without ever looking in the rear view mirror. In fact, I was rarely present long enough to allow something to become a memory once it was behind me. My intense focus was on the future and the goals I was hell-bent on accomplishing. My eyes were lifted toward the grand prize in the sky that I envisioned would somehow be bestowed upon me if I just accomplished enough...the prize of finally becoming 'somebody' in this life.

Unfortunately, when you're in a rut of dissatisfaction like I was, positive memories are often difficult to make and even harder to remember.

Through my own life launch, I've started to understand the power of being in the moment and fully experiencing the sights, sounds, smells, and emotions of a particular season of life. There is a richness and beauty that every hour of life holds, and the question is whether or not I'm aware of it and can embrace it for what it's worth.

There were times in my life when I was physically *and* emotionally present though.

Like when I was seven years old and opened my new-fangled, gold(en) watch on Christmas Eve...or when my dad and I went to every basketball game at the local university across the street from our house…or when I played sports with the same kids all the way through elementary school…or like most mornings when my mom made me breakfast from the time I was born until I left for college.

Those positive memories are lodged in a special place and sealed with a warmth that won't allow them to fade away. *If we allow them to, our memories can point us toward the life we really want.*

You have memories like that, don't you? These are positive, life-giving memories of your past that are road markers pointing you toward that which you cherish.

When we're able to tap into the goodness of those moments, we can extract what is nourishing and beautiful about life. We start to get a sense of the satisfying, meaningful life that we really want.

Of course, you and I both have negative recollections as well. These are experiences along the path we'd rather forget, but it's good that we haven't. Those memories play a role, too. They are warning signs of what to avoid or at least how to navigate through treacherous terrain if and when we encounter it once again.

The Good Ole Days
You should know that I'm an only child who spent a great deal of meaningful time with my parents over the years, but they now live six or so hours away in Sacramento…essentially worlds apart from my southern California lifestyle. When we do get together, we'll undoubtedly find ourselves in the midst of conversation saying, "Remember when…"

My wife rolls her eyes, and my kids head out of the room. They know what's about to commence…a warm-hearted reminiscing of the good ole days.

Because my parents grew up in Alabama and I spent my youth in Kentucky, there is a certain level of sappiness that's connected to all things 'southern.' We love southern food, southern hospitality, southern accents, and southern college sports...especially anything to do with Louisville basketball and Alabama football. And, one of our favorite topics is all our southern relatives.

"Remember when Pa-Pa pulled the fishing net back onto the pier and it had a stingray in it?" I reflect on my grandfather hoisting a giant casting net off the Fairhope Pier in southern Alabama.

"Yeeesss, you were in awe of that thang," my Mom smiles.

"I remember his long, gray beard shining in the bright sun as he taught me how to sort the fish and shrimp. What ever happened to those nets?"

"Well, I guess they were sold in a yard sale after he died." The conversation lulls with an impromptu moment of silence.

Good memories...they take you back to a time when things were sweet and beautiful and oftentimes...simpler.

Why is that scene locked in my mind's eye?

Could it be the wonder and awe of doing something for the first time? Maybe it was the love of my grandfather? Or, perhaps it was the fact that I had no care in the world other than enjoying the moment?

Whatever the reason is, I'll never forget that day. I'll never forget the stingray or my Pa-Pa or the cool breeze blowing through his long gray beard.

Our conversations seem to meander into the same cul-de-sacs of memories over and over again. It's like those memories mean something more than the rest...as if they're locked into place more firmly than the others.

My family and I moved from Kentucky to California in between my sophomore and junior years in high school, and the experience of traveling cross-country was enough to destroy (or solidify) any average family. In our case, it did the latter. We still laugh about getting our car stereo stolen the first week we arrived in the Golden State.

I love to mimic the officer who came out to write the report. Sticking out my chest and grabbing my make-believe gun holster, I lower my voice, "Welcome to California, folks!"

"I'll never forget Dandie screeching in the back of the station wagon as we drove through Texas…" I reminisce about our one-eyed cat that wasn't exactly the poster-pet for a cross-country move.

"I knooow. He was not happy at all to be traveling in the dark hours of the early mornin'!" my Mom laughs out loud.

"Remember when our dog pooped in the back, and Dandie started howling…I thought Dad was gonna go nuts. He was freakin' out!"

"I was *not* freakin' out. It was your mother who was dying from the smell that dog left all the way in the back of the car."

Laughter bellows through the room, and my wife tries to join in as best she can…but she really can't…not truly. Those aren't her memories. Although she can be gracious and enter into them at some level, they're really the memories of those who were present. They mean something to us…they are special…they are sacred.

Remember… if we allow them to, our memories can point us toward the life we really want.

As we unearth these recollections, we'll be able to see what was meaningful and important to us then…and what can lead us to a satisfying life in the here and now.

Although organic conversations allow memories to unfold spontaneously, I want to invite you to take an intentional journey back in time to excavate what's been waiting to be discovered within you. Along the way, you'll come across memories that are playful, powerful, and painful. They're all part of your life, and we all have them. Take a deep breath and know that I'm with you in the process.

1. Take time to reflect on the journey of your life.

Allow your mind's eye to travel back in time. Journey toward your earliest memories. Are they of your mom and dad or siblings or someone else? What were you doing? Can you see what you were wearing?

Now...grow a little older in your mind. Do you remember those special days as a kid? Days of playing outside with your brother or sister or friends? What games did you play? What did you talk about? Was there innocence to it all?

As you matured, can you remember times of adventure? How about beauty? When did you feel peaceful and at ease? Can you close your eyes and see moments full of love? How about when you first felt the transcendent presence of the Divine?

If you're having a hard time remembering your past, maybe you'll find it helpful to pull out an old photo album or scroll through some images on your computer. Maybe you'd like to flip through a high school yearbook or read through an old journal. Find an open door to your mind's eye and the depths of your heart that will allow you access to these precious memories of years gone by.

2. Remember when you felt most alive.

Now that you've taken a meandering journey through the past, I want to ask you to focus in on times when you felt most energized. It doesn't matter how old or young you were. Just allow your heart to lead you to a specific moment or season of life when you were thriving in some way.

Although most of us envision 'thriving' in the form of external success (getting A's in school, graduating from college, or getting a new job), perhaps the thriving was more internal. Maybe it wasn't a time in your life when you were outwardly thriving. Maybe you were thriving in the face of adversity.

What did it feel like? Did it feel like adrenaline was pumping through your veins? Or, was it an aura of peacefulness? Perhaps you were energetic and vigorous…

As you see yourself in the past, were you smiling, laughing, and playing? Were you alone or with a large group? What did your body language say about your experience of the moment?

3. Remember when you felt most empty.

I know it may not be much fun, but I'd like to challenge you to do the same thing with times when life felt barren or hollow. To feel empty means that there was something lacking.

Think about a time when you were not only lacking something outwardly…but inwardly.

When was a time when you lacked peace? A time when you felt so stressed or anxious or burdened down. How about a season when you were without close friends or family who would stand with you? Sure, they may have been physically present, but you felt alone and without community.

How about a job where you didn't feel like your gifts, talents, and passions were being fully utilized? What about a situation among a group of people where your thoughts or feelings weren't valued?

You'll never forget those times, will you? They serve a purpose if you'll allow them to. These painful memories will direct you away from possible danger and give you compassion for those experiencing similar situations.

4. What can you learn about the life you've always wanted?

Now that you've taken a journey through the memories of your heart, what can you learn? Why have those memories (which probably include the full gamut of feelings) been solidified within you while so many others have simply faded away?

Perhaps you were more present in these moments and experienced the subtle textures of life. Or, could it be that these memories hold a depth of meaning that other more mundane moments have not?

In the midst of the memories when you felt most alive, what were you doing? I don't necessarily mean the actual physical activity… I mean the underlying essence of the moment.

For instance, I remember crouching down in my backyard on Nutwood Avenue in Bowling Green, Kentucky, with a pocketknife in my hand. I had just climbed off the nailed-in wooden steps that led up to a perch in the crook of a large tree providing a giant umbrella of shade. As my feet hit the dusty dirt, I bent down to pick up a broken branch that I had cast aside days before.

I whipped open the knife, and I start whittling down the wood just like Pa-Pa had shown me a few weeks prior. I switched to my left hand, and I grasped the wood tightly with my right. As the knife scraped across the wood, it slipped and landed squarely on the top of my right index finger. Blood instantly squirted out all over the knife, wood, and my brand new t-shirt.

Without shedding a tear, I casually walked inside and got a paper towel to wrap around my finger.

"Mom, I cut myself!" I proudly announced.

It was my first time…and I did it with my own knife while whittling a piece of wood. I wasn't embarrassed. I was *thrilled*. There was a sense of adventure, danger, and excitement that came from the moment.

As I look down at my finger right now, I'm proud to see that scar so vividly present. It's a memory of a simpler time when it was okay to take risks. It was exciting to be adventurous and experiment with things for the first time.

What happened to that part of me?

Maybe that child-like adventurer grew up and became an adult. Maybe I had to start playing it safe and do the responsible thing.

Maybe…or maybe not. It is conceivable that I lost that edge of risk, and it's part of the life I've always wanted. For all one knows, that's one of the reasons why I made some irresponsible decisions as an adult. What if I had given myself permission to be adventurous all along? What if I found ways to experiment with life in ways that embraced both freedom *and* responsibility?

How about you? Can you see the underlying theme as you remember your most 'alive' moments? Are you able to envision your passions in life as you reminisce about how you spent your free time when you didn't have to be a productive adult every waking moment?

And, what clues can you ascertain from those times when you felt most empty? Were you immature and unable to handle the difficult experience? Or, was the emptiness a clue that you shouldn't move in that direction over the course of your life? Have you learned from those experiences?

As I walked through the process of re-launching my own life, I found that these memories became like close friends. They acted as a Divine Whisper beckoning me down the road that seemed to be more lit than others. They pointed me in the direction of *life*…not a life based on the past…but a life based on what had been uniquely created within me.

I found that as I recalled these meaningful experiences, my unique perspective and passion for life emerged. It had been there all along…just waiting to be discovered.

During a recent visit to my parent's home, my mom led me out into the garage to peruse two stacks of clear, plastic tubs filled with keepsakes from my growing-up years. I cracked open the first lid to discover everything that was left inside my desk I didn't need on the day I left for college. There was a tub filled with virtually every uniform I wore on sports teams during elementary school and junior high. I found my baseball card collection and yearbooks and even the 1970s NFL sheets from my childhood bed.

No, my mom is not a hoarder...she's just proud of her only son.

As we left on Sunday afternoon, I loaded about half of the boxes into the back of our van to dig through once we got home...sort of like archeological treasures from my past. The flood of emotions was unending as I reminisced about each and every item. My wife nodded her head to convey some level of understanding for about 15 minutes, but that's all she could take.

I was mesmerized how this unanticipated time capsule could open up such a wealth of clues about the life I really wanted.

So often, we look upon mementos of the past as nothing more than childish rubbish that's glazed over with sentimentality. Yet, if we're willing to look beyond the layer of dust and yellowish, dog-eared corners, we'll find underlying meaning that is priceless.

When I saved all this stuff...was it because I was sentimental, or was it because there was a passion inside of me to document what I had experienced so I could share it with others? Was the collection of college basketball programs all about the team...or more about my relationship with my dad? Were the photographs all about my love for photography...or more about my passion to capture precious moments?

Are you starting to see how the past can be a road marker that leads to an *alive* future? Can you envision how your memories shine a light to help you walk out of the rut of dissatisfaction you can easily fall into?

You have that light within you.

Are you willing to aim it into the corners of your life?
Are you willing to slow down and reflect on what's holding you back?
Are you willing to discover what's possible in your future?
.

What If?
chapter 03

As I was growing up, my parents and I took numerous family trips together. Notice I said 'family' and 'trips'...come to find out neither of which add up to an actual vacation. Sure, they called them vacations, but they were lying.

Instead, we went to places like Warrior, Alabama, and Gulfport, Mississippi...fine places to visit...but not so much to 'vacation.' I'd come home from Spring Break and hear about other kids in my class who went to places like Hilton Head and Panama City and even this place called California. Although I loved many of the down-home experiences I gained, you can't tell me that a vacation includes sleeping on the floor at your relatives' house and exploring the 'crick' that runs behind it.

It's not as though my parents didn't want to take a vacation, but spending money on that sort of thing just wasn't a priority...nor something their parents did with them. They preferred to ensure we had a roof over our heads and food on the dinner table and shoes on my feet...which I am extremely thankful for.

Without even realizing it, I automatically assumed that vacations were for 'other' people, and spending money on travel (unless you're going to see your relatives) was frivolous.

It wasn't until our first few years of marriage that my wife started trying to talk me into going on a trip that didn't involve seeing her parents or mine.

"Babe, our anniversary is coming up, and I'd really like to go someplace fun…"

"Like where?" I asked…already with an air of suspicion.

"Liiiiike…Hawaii!"

Her family has been there on several occasions…for no special reason at all. I hardly believed it when she told me. I thought for sure she had a long lost relative that died, and they just went over there for the funeral. She assured me that it was completely just for fun.

"Hawaii? Are you crazy? You know how much that would cost us!?!"

"Yes, and it'll be worth it. We're creating memories."

"Honey, we can create some memories right here at home," I hinted.

She rolled her eyes, but I didn't give in.

Although we took a week-long, budget-minded honeymoon to Boston (for less than $2,000), we hadn't taken any other significant trips since then. My lack of desire to spend money on 'frivolous' travel combined with my workaholic tendencies created blinders that prevented me from seeing any other perspective.

Frankly, I didn't know any different.

I had never experienced the freedom of enjoying a lazy walk on an exotic beach, savoring a pricey meal in a faraway place, or exploring off the beaten paths of a foreign culture.

If you haven't ever experienced something, it's hard to even imagine what it would be like.

Sometimes it takes hearing the experiences of others and seeing photos in order to finally say "what if?" For me, it was a combination of the two. I started hearing about the adventures of other couples who set aside money to take a vacation at least once a year...somewhere other than the home of a relative. On top of that, I'd notice the joy on their faces upon their return as well as their smile-filled photos that covered their coffee table.

"Hmm....what if we took a trip like that?" I started to wonder. "Maybe, we'd have that much fun. Maybe the financial investment would be worth it."

I finally relented, and my wife and I took our first cruise together. It was the experience of close friends that served as my personal brochure... just enough to allow me to say "what if?"

By the time I walked on board for a quick 3-day getaway down the coast of Baja, I was sold. The smell of the salty sea, the plethora of food choices, and the cozy cabins...I was ready to live there!

Notice I said 'first' cruise. We loved it so much that we've taken a couple of more, and we've travelled all sorts of places together and as a family...even as far away as India and Dubai for two weeks over Christmas break...with both of our kids!

I needed to get to a place where I was open to envisioning a new way of life. Because the thought of spending money on a trip conflicted with my experience in childhood, I had such a difficult time seeing the benefit. It was like trying to shove an entire cruise ship into my brain. It just wasn't going to happen until I was ready to dream what my life could look like with a new experience.

What. If.

The same thing is true about all aspects of life...not just vacations (which

I thoroughly enjoy now).

If you can't catch a vision for your life…
If you can't imagine a new normal…
If you can't see that there are other possibilities…
Your experience will remain the same.

You'll keep walking down the same road when you could be experiencing a life-changing adventure.

Believing in Possibilities

You'd think that as we get older our minds would broaden with possibilities, but I'm finding that it's usually just the opposite. From the moment my son began to talk, he's been constantly using those same two words. What. If.

"What if…there was a car that could fly over all this traffic? And, what if you didn't even have to drive it? What if it drove itself? What if you just pushed a button and it just flew there? What if that was possible, Daddy?"

"Yes, Emerson…what if?"

My wife and I will often look over at each other as our son "what ifs" from the backseat and smile at one another. His mind seems to be missing the limitations that most of us have put in place. He isn't triggered by any certain topic. It's not as if he's hyper-focused on dinosaurs or video games or newborn animals he sees on TV.

It could be anything.

His eyes are a giant funnel through which he takes in this glorious world that he's lived in for seven short years. With few barriers to his mind, these visuals penetrate the permeable membranes of his gray matter, and his synapses start firing immediately. Anything is up for grabs…there is no telling what he may come up with. It could be a possibility involving people, places, or pets. It may focus on the sky above or the ocean be-

What If? 37

low. No matter what it is, if something intrigues him with possibilities, it's likely to come spilling out of his mouth in the form of a question.

He doesn't ask very many questions about how something works or what we're doing for the day or even when we'll finally arrive at our destination. He inquires about *possibilities*.

His questions don't require much of an answer...and yet they're not necessarily rhetorical either. They're questions that beg for affirmation. He's looking for, "Yes, I can imagine that!"

It's clear that he doesn't have it all figured out, and that's the beauty of his inquiries. If he actually tried to nail down all the details before he brought it to our attention, he'd never ask those two small words...*what if?*

We're not born with those limitations, are we?

We're not born with mental barriers pre-installed at varying distances within our minds that prevent us from exploring the unknown. Sure, some of us are more inquisitive than others...but something happens along the way of life. In our early years, a well-meaning adult wants to protect us from the pain of disappointment and unmet expectations... usually the safety-conscious parent between the two.

I could have responded in a kind, yet fatherly tone, "Oh, Emerson... that's so cute! You have such a wild imagination...but cars will *never* fly!"

Or, in my worst moments, "Can you please quit asking so many questions?!? Can't you see that I'm trying to find this restaurant? I need to focus on the road!"

Once a child has most of the possibilities squeezed out of them – either through an appeasing pat on the head or unending shame that lands them in a therapist's office years later – they've learned the lesson that everything isn't possible in this world. Then, they start to reinforce this notion in other children...teasing the creative types that they should come back down to reality.

If you're perturbed by this sort of creative mind-wandering, my guess is that you're muttering under your breath, "Well...I'm simply a realist."

Yes, you are. You are realistic about what can and can't happen in this world, and I'm not speaking to you. I'm addressing the 10% of people who haven't given up on the belief that there are unending possibilities. I'm focused on those of you who believe in what others see as impossible.

As I was growing up, I had this sense that I could become anything I wanted to be in this world. I could be a garbage man (kindergarten), a professional basketball player (7th grade), a photographer (high school), or a pastor (college).

And, at some point along the way, I picked up a statement to test my belief in limitless possibilities. I would say to myself, "I can be the President of the United States...if I really want to be."

The role of President is practically impossible for most people to attain in our country. Yet, the day that I start believing that it's impossible for me is the day that I've stopped believing in possibilities.

In reality, I don't *want* to be the President. It doesn't align with my mission in this life, but it does test my mind for what I believe is possible. Do you have an outlandish possibility that would help to test your beliefs?

Apathy Will Kill You
If you're going to experience a life launch, the power of possibilities will be one of your greatest assets. You'll need to have an open mind and heart to what is possible in situations that seem like a big mess and have little chance of turning around.

Think about your family and friends. What's the condition of your relationships? Are your kids functioning as part of the family unit or just doing their own thing? Do you enjoy being together or are you merely roommates? What do you see?

How about your job? Are you just in it for the money or is there a passion? Do you really want to be doing something else, but you're just too scared to make a move? Or, are you even aware of what you are passionate about?

Think about other areas of your life…like your physical health, romance, spirituality, and finances. What do you see?

I see possibilities.

If you see problems without possibilities, you'll end up on the sidelines of life without being part of the solution. My guess is that you'll find yourself feeling…

> **Hopeless** – Without possibilities, we feel as though there's no way out. We may keep going through the motions of life, but we give up inside.
>
> **Suspicious** – We think that people just want to take something from us. Rather than seeing that we have an opportunity to invest, we're concerned that someone is just scamming us out of what's rightfully our own.
>
> **Stuck** – If we can't see that transformation is possible, we'll quit moving forward. We'll find ourselves unable (or unwilling) to take a next step in relationships.
>
> **Worried** – Instead of focusing on taking proactive steps toward a solution, it will be easy to meditate on all the negative things that could possibly go wrong. Rather than looking at the positive possibilities, we're allowing all the negative ones to swirl around in our brains.

That's why asking "what if?" and believing in unending possibilities is so important. If you believe that nothing can be done (in a particular area of your life), then you'll end up in the land of apathy. That's where most of us live, isn't it?

Instead of living in the realm of possibilities, we build a comfy estate in Apathyville, and we're satisfied to live like we've always lived... oftentimes following in the footsteps of our parents. We go to work, make money, buy stuff, and live for the weekend. We try to keep our relationships void of any conflict, but we don't hardly get to know our own neighbors...much less invest at a depth that develops real intimacy. We somehow buy into the lie that passion is for people who have a lot of time on their hands. We seem to be more interested in marathon DVR sessions than thinking deeply about the intentions of our lives.

Apathy is simply the recognition of a need, challenge, or problem without any intention or motivation to be part of the transformation. Frankly, it's killing us. It's robbing us of the life we've always wanted.

What Kind of Life Do You Want?

Although we'll delve deeply into each one of The Seven Spheres of Transformation later on, now is the time to start to get a mental picture of the life you really want. This isn't the life that the magazine ads want you to have...or the people who make the movies with the mood-altering music scored on top of them.

This is your life.

As many of us update the world with a mere 144 characters on Twitter or a few more on Facebook, the reality is that the whole of your life will come down to just about that many characters. Have you ever thought of life that way? The whole of your life will come down to 144 (or less) characters that are etched onto your tombstone.

Oftentimes, the best place to begin is with the end in mind.

What do you want your tombstone to say about you? Unless you leave it in your will, your family members will decide for you. What do you want them to highlight?

- Your accumulation of stuff?
- Your overworking to get that next title?
- Your passion for your family?
- Your heart for those in need?

If you were to look at the way you invest your time, talents, and money right now, what do you think your tombstone should say about you? Are you happy with that? Do you want it to say something different?

The great thing is that you've got time to change. No matter how young or old you are, you can begin making adjustments today. You simply have to keep the end in mind. Otherwise, you're likely to launch a life that someone else wants you to have.

Here's what I envision for *my* life.

I'm 99 years old (because I plan to live to 100), and I'm lying in a comfortable bed that adjusts up and down (because I've always wanted one of those). I am surrounded by my two children who are in their 70s along with my grandchildren and great grandchildren and maybe even some great, great grandchildren. I have a smile on my face as I look around the room at the heritage I have left behind for each one of them.

The heritage isn't about money...although I envision that all their needs have been provided for. The heritage is about a love that's rooted in our faith in God. It's about loving the One who created us and loving our fellow humankind...especially those who are broken and in need. As I look around the room, I see the generosity of their hearts that is practically lived out in their everyday lives...through their vocations, through their financial investment, and even through the kindness of their words.

I foresee our relationships being intimate and connecting. It's not to say that there hasn't been conflict, but we've been committed to work through it. We've been focused on the well-being of one another and not on the selfish reactions that come from bruising one another. I see love, faithfulness, and courage.

How about you? What do you see? How do you envision the final days of your life will be spent? Who will be with you? What will they say?

How about the people who hear of your death? Will they recognize your name? What will be their impression of your life?

Once you get a mental picture of the end, you can begin to work your way backwards. It's not as though that picture will actually come true (although it may). It's more about setting the trajectory of your intention in that direction. If you allow the winds and waves of life to push you back and forth, you'll just flop around in the giant washing machine of life. But, if you really want to have a life that's characterized by true success, you'll take time to reflect upon the life you truly want.

In light of how it will all come to an end, what do you need to begin doing now in order to see that come to fruition?

- **Who do you want to be?**
  A life doesn't begin with behavior (or doing)…it begins with our internal world of being. It involves our thoughts, attitudes, and feelings. Your 'being' flows out of what you choose to cultivate inside your mind and heart.

- **How would you like to invest the days of your life?**
  You have a choice as to how you'll invest your time. This is the only opportunity that you'll have to live today. However you chose to spend your day…you literally chose to exchange 24 hours for those experiences. You 'spent' the currency of time in order to receive those experiences. Are you happy with your investment?

- **How would you like to utilize your financial resources?**
  Based on the financial resources you have (whether large or small), are you satisfied with the way you're utilizing it? Do you find that you're disappointed in what you're getting in return for your

money? Would you like to begin investing it in a different way?

- **How will you treat people in your life?**
  Each and every one of us interacts with people on a daily basis. The way you treat those people is a direct indication of what you think about them. If you value them in your life, you'll be loving...patient, kind, and generous. If you see them as mere pawns in the game of your life, you'll move them around and use them in order to get what you want.

- **How will you deal with conflict?**
  Whenever two individuals spend a significant amount of time together, conflict is inevitable. Each of us have different opinions, perspectives, and preferences. Those will conflict at some point. How will you handle that scenario? By yelling and arguing? By discussing it thoughtfully and personally? Or, by simply avoiding it altogether?

- **What role will reflection and learning play?**
  Learning isn't automatic. It requires focus and a desire to ascertain knowledge from an experience. If you're going to intentionally move toward a mental picture of your preferable future, ongoing learning is needed to continue to direct your heart toward what you truly want in life.

These questions are meant to massage your mind to the point that a mental picture starts to form...an image of the life you want to end up with. Ironically, by creating the image itself, you'll start to live it. Your intentions will begin to come into alignment with your desired life, and you'll begin to make new choices based on what you see.

The mental picture will give you the power to ask the question, "What if?" What if I started to invest my time in a new way? What if I began to treat people like a valuable, uniquely created life? What if I lived with the end in mind? What if?

The Process of Intention
section 2

After abruptly ending my 10 years of workaholism, I enjoyed the ecstasy of an affair and the beginning of a brand new life...a life I could create from the ground up. This mystical life wouldn't continue. In fact, it was unrealistic to think that the 'high' I was experiencing would be long-lasting. Even if this woman and I had stayed together, our relationship would have required a shift from daily dates to the natural rhythms of an intimacy-developing relationship.

Fortunately...she left me.

I didn't feel that way at the time. In fact, I was utterly devastated...even to the point of battling suicide. Her departure forced me to ask some tough questions that I'm not sure I would have been willing to ask otherwise. I definitely wasn't willing to ask them before leaving my wife to have the affair, and I'm not sure I would have had much motivation to ask them while I was reveling in the euphoria of an illicit relationship.

After checking out of the hospital and continuing to battle depression and suicide for two weeks, I finally came to a place of deep remorse. I was ready to apologize to my wife and ask for her forgiveness…perhaps she would be able to extend it at some point in the future. Although I wasn't necessarily interested in getting back together with her, I just knew that the life I truly wanted involved making amends with those who I had betrayed…starting with my family.

It was the devastation of hitting rock bottom that called for me to ask some deep, dark questions most of us never want to ask. These questions require us to look at who we are, what we want, and how we can ultimately experience it. The process isn't started with a Scantron form and a #2 pencil. It begins by taking a slow, thoughtful look within your own soul.

We jump from thought to conclusion so rapidly in our culture that it's helpful to put our thinking into slow motion for this process. It's imperative that we take each step with careful consideration to ensure we're seeing how each thought interconnects with the others…creating new intentions that ultimately produce a new normal.

Remember, intentionality is at the heart of every life launch. Without a high level of intention, you'll simply continue experiencing the life that you've always had. May these five questions slow your thinking down to the point that you can hear a Whisper directing your next steps.

Who Am I?
chapter 04

Although the current Space Shuttle program is winding down, I remember when it was first starting to take off. As a nine year old, my eyes were glued to the television set in our living room as I saw the replay on the evening news. Although my imagination could believe in a rocket circling our globe, it was unbelievable to actually see a 122-foot long spacecraft being propelled with such fiery force.

Does the Shuttle need a license plate?
How do they pull that thing up to a gas pump?
When do the astronauts get to go to the bathroom?
(All questions going through my young mind.)

Most of us are so enamored by the construction or power of the Shuttle that we rarely even think about the pad from which it launches. Have you ever stopped to think about the strength and depth of the foundation of the launch pad itself?

In order for the rocket boosters to launch the Shuttle over 200 miles above the Earth and ultimately orbit at over 17,000 miles per hour, the foundation for lift-off must be as carefully constructed as any other component. Can you imagine trying to prop up a giant spacecraft next to a rickety, wooden launch pad placed on top of a sandy layer of dirt?

The whole thing would simply fall over, and it would be a tremendous waste of time and money. Without a strong foundation, the launch of the Shuttle wouldn't even be possible.

The truth is that if you're planning to launch your life beyond where you find yourself now, you'll need to ensure that you have a solid foundation from which to propel.

In life, that foundation is your identity.

The Foundation of Our Lives
After the three-day hospital visit, I knew I just couldn't return to the apartment we had leased and moved into together. It was too painful to walk back into the place that we had called home for six short weeks. I *had* to move.

Because most of my friends had distanced themselves from me during the most tumultuous time in my life, I decided to move 30 minutes away to be close to two friends who were willing to walk with me through this process. I packed up all the stuff that had been accumulated in such a short time, and I leased another apartment in Newport Beach.

The accommodations were nice, and the complex was quite sprawling… a well-equipped exercise room, two pools, tennis courts, and basketball hoops…all things that I had little or no use for during the last 10 years of working constantly. Day after day, I'd wake up with nothing to do.

I had no job.
I had no appointments.
I had very little money.
I had a couple of friends.
I had a small amount of time with my kids each week.
And, I had no goals for my life.
(All things that used to give me an identity.)

I take that back…my goal was just to make it through the day.

Some of you probably feel that way right now. Perhaps you didn't quit your job or leave your spouse, but you've contemplated that possibility. Maybe you'd never actually have the guts to pull the trigger, but you've been thinking about it deep inside.

The reason why you're just trying to make it through your day or week or life is because you're *stuck*...stuck with something you don't want.

Rather than loading the rocket of your life on the launch pad and blowing the whole thing up, begin by re-thinking the foundation from the very start...before you make any other moves.

Although I wish I could have asked this question with depth before I blew up my own life, I started asking it during those days when I had absolutely nothing to do. The answers didn't come through some mystical, cosmic experience (i.e., the voice of God) or by reading a book or even seeing a therapist.

The answer came by exploring my own identity.
Who am I?

There are four aspects of your identity that will ensure a solid foundation as you become intentional about the way you are living.

1. Your Divine Imprint

After retiring from 30 years in the Navy, my grandfather became an incredible woodworker – creating everything from toy cars, skateboards, and even a giant, oak roll-top desk for each of his children and grandchildren. With each item he handcrafted, he placed an imprint (burned into the wood) that read "Handcrafted by Erskine B. Trotter."

It was hidden in a place that wouldn't be readily seen if you were utilizing the object. The imprint wasn't about getting credit for his creation...it was about designating the object as 'one of a kind' and special. He wanted people to know that it wasn't made at a conveyor-belt factory...even as people use the item years later.

In the same way that my grandfather's character is seen in the pieces he created, you can see the qualities of the One who created humankind as you look deeply into your own life.

A divine imprint is that part of humankind that reveals a great deal about why we were created and what we're created for. This imprint isn't easy to see if you're not accustomed to looking for it…often mistaken as merely the way humans adapted to living in this world.

We've been imprinted with an ability to love and be loved…created for *relationships*. We're not robots or drones. Instead, we have the ability to connect with other human beings in a rich and meaningful way.

You and I also have the ability to reflect, learn, and *make decisions* about our lives. We're not living under the heavy hand of a Master Puppeteer nor are we flopping around without the potential to act upon an intention. We have the power to choose a direction for our lives.

And, we have been empowered to *create* in this life. Our minds are fashioned in such a way that creativity can inform how we use our hands to build and construct.

These deeply-embedded abilities are just a few of the ways we've been given an imprint that points to the One who created us and sustains us. If we want a firm grasp on our identity, we'd be served well to continue reflecting on Who created us and for what reason beyond our simple enjoyment of this life.

2. Your Strengths

You have a natural propensity toward certain activities, and these 'strengths' are unique to you. You have a combination of strong points that only you possess. No one else is exactly like you.

If you have brothers or sisters, it was very clear to you during your growing up years that they were stronger than you in certain ways. Perhaps, you were disappointed by the fact that they excelled in sports while you struggled...or they got good grades while you had to study extra hard. On the other hand, you probably gloated when it became apparent that you were able to outperform them in some other activity.

I can see the uniqueness of strengths play out in my own children. Emerson, 7 years old, is quite adept at navigating his way around the home computer...playing all sorts of online games. On the other hand, Waverly, age 11, is a writer who can come up with rich stories that capture the imagination. We don't try to make Emerson be just like Waverly or Waverly to excel in areas where Emerson is apparently stronger. We highlight the strengths of each child and cheer them on...knowing that they are both unique human beings.

Think about your own strengths for a moment.

What do you have a natural disposition toward? Are you gifted in using your hands to create or fix things? Do you cook and serve those around you with grace and ease? Or, maybe you are passionate about numbers and they just come easy for you.

There are an endless amount of strengths in this life, and you have been given many of them believe it or not. Don't buy into the lie that you aren't strong at anything...or something of significance. That's just not the case.

You were created with gifts, talents, and inclinations that can be nurtured and developed even further. There's very little sense in focusing on your weaknesses and trying to turn those into strengths. I've never seen anyone do that. Sure, you'd be wise to minimize those weaknesses, but your real focus should be on those areas where you're uniquely gifted.

If you don't know what they are, you'd be well served to start asking people who are close to you. Tell them that you're trying to discover your strengths so that you can maximize and build upon them. A true friend will be happy to encourage you in this way.

By focusing on the places in your life where you're already strong, don't be surprised when you increase your effectiveness double, quadruple, or even a hundredfold.

3. Your Wiring

Not only do we each have unique strengths, but we also have a particular 'wiring' or personality. The way you are wired is a combination of qualities that make you uniquely you. While strengths tend to be geared toward certain outward activities, your wiring is the internal realm that determines how you approach the world around you.

There are numerous personality profile tests that can help you learn more about how you're wired from the inside out. Here are three popular ones...

Myers Briggs Type Indicator – outlines 16 distinct personality types.

DISC – uses the four dimensions of Dominance, Influence, Steadiness, and Conscientiousness.

Personality Plus – focuses on four types including Choleric, Melancholy, Sanguine, and Phlegmatic.

None of the personality profiles used within any of these tests are specifically described as positive or negative. It must be understood that there are upsides and downsides to all of them. The purpose of the process is to observe and identify...not to judge or pigeonhole someone into only functioning in one particular way. Remember that we are fluid human beings who can choose many different methods of interaction, but we do have a certain wiring that is most prominent.

While the Myers Briggs Type Indicator is seen as more thorough, Personality Plus is one of the easier profiles to quickly assimilate…especially to understand how different personalities relate with one another. Although the profile is administered through a series of questions, perhaps you can pick out which personality most resembles your wiring through a simple overview.

If you are a *Choleric*, you're usually focused on getting things done and can accidentally run over people in the process. You can be both decisive and stubborn. Cholerics are leaders who are passionate about their vision.

A *Melancholy* is a highly talented person who develops brilliant ideas. They can often paralyze themselves with over-analysis. If you are a Melancholy, you are passionate about lists and doing things the 'right way.'

If you are a *Sanguine*, you get along well with people and can get others excited about your interests. Unfortunately, you can't always be relied upon to get things done…especially the details. You love being with others and play the role of the entertainer in group interactions. You may have a tendency to over-promise and under-deliver.

Finally, a *Phlegmatic* is stable and most neutral. Although you may not actively upset people, your indifference may frustrate those around you. You are comfortable not making decisions and generally fine with the status quo. You care about the harmony of the people around you.

A simplification might be that a Choleric likes it my way, a Melancholy likes it the right way, a Sanguine likes it the fun way, and a Phlegmatic likes it the easy way.

The truth is that you are wired uniquely and beautifully, and it is part of the foundation of your identity.

4. Your Story

Not only do we each have unique strengths and wiring, but we also have a 'one of a kind' story to our lives. Some of us are younger, and our stories are rather short. Others of us are more mature, and there are more years behind us than in front of us.

No matter what…your story is *your* story. It is no more or less important than the journey anyone else has taken.

Although our stories include the ordinary times of life, the narrative is most defined by the highs and lows we experience along the way. If you think back on your life, most of what you will remember will be those times when you experienced something extremely exhilarating or profoundly painful. These seasons (however long or short) compel you to define your story.

It's interesting to note that two different people can go through a similar situation, but the story they tell themselves is quite different. Two friends may go through a layoff at a large corporation. One takes on the role of a martyr while the other sees it as an opportunity. Two people…two different stories.

Being aware of the story that you're telling yourself is helpful in developing your own identity. Although you may not be able to change the experiences you've had or the choices you've made, you can choose to see it all in different ways.

Were painful experiences the result of someone being against you? Or, are they an opportunity to experience transformation and growth?

Was your parent's choice to sell the family home a hair-brained move? Or, can you see it as an opportunity to experience flexibility?

Most of these re-frames are possible as we look back upon the painful experiences we've walked through. It's not dismissing the pain, but it is seeing the events from a different angle, which may cause your story to take a different twist.

Be aware that your story may inform someone of your past, but your story does not necessarily define your future. There are endless possibilities to learn from the past so that you can embrace the days ahead with passion and focus.

You are not a victim of your story. Without minimizing anything, you can re-define it along the way. It's part of your identity…your foundation…and you can make it as weak or strong as you'd like.

Sand or Stone…It's Your Choice

The more you are aware of your divine imprint, strengths, wiring, and story…the greater opportunity you'll have to develop a strong foundation for your life. Without a strong launch pad, you'll try to make significant changes, but they won't be grounded in much at all.

In the end, this will be nothing more than an effort in behavior management. You'll make a change on the outside (polishing up the rocket of your life), but there won't be much substance to launch from. It's the difference between propping your life up on a foundation of shaky sand or launching from a firm foundation that's rock solid and unshakable.

How about you? As you're in the process of a life launch, what type of foundation are you building upon? Sand or stone? Here are a few ways to ensure that you have a strong foundation for this process…

- **Discover your divine imprint.**
  Be willing to ask the question, "Why am I here?"…and listen. Although you may not have a conclusive answer right away, the mere process of asking will create a strength to your life.

- **Embrace your strengths (and weaknesses).**
  Make a list of all your strengths and non-strengths. The more you embrace both of these…the stronger your foundation will get. You won't feel the need to be more or less than who you are. That's

called humility. When someone points out one of your weaknesses, you can readily admit, "Yep, that's one of my non-strengths." There's nothing personal about it. It's not an attack. Do you know why? Because you've already embraced it. *And*, when someone else is succeeding in life, you won't have a need to criticize or pull him or her down. Why? Because you're comfortable knowing that you are strong and successful yourself.

- **Uncover your hard wiring.**
  Your personality is beautiful and broken...all at the same time. You are not perfect, and you'll be miserable if you try to act like those not-so-fun parts of your personality aren't there. Uncover it all. Get comfortable with it. It's part of who you are. Celebrate who you've been uniquely created to be...and minimize those aspects of your wiring that cause difficulty and pain.

- **Trace your story.**
  Pull out a piece a paper and trace the highs and lows of your life from the beginning to the present. As you look back, what were the events, experiences, and seasons that shaped you the most? What story are you telling yourself about your own life? Do you like that story? Or, would you like to re-frame it in some way?

As you've probably figured out, the process of ensuring a firm foundation isn't overnight or a one-time occurrence. This is something that continues to be discovered and embraced over the course of your life.

When I spend time with my grandparents or others who are in the final two-thirds of their life, I'm able to see the strength that comes from this process. If someone has been willing to wrestle through difficult questions of life, there is a strength in their identity that's remarkable. They are comfortable with who they are, and they're not out to prove anything. They encourage others to be themselves, and they cheer people on to succeed.

No matter what age you find yourself right now, the more you become comfortable with answering the question, "Who am I?"...the stronger your life launch will be. And, when something goes haywire down the road, you can remind yourself of the greatness that is within you.

What Do I Want?
chapter 05

We all want something in this life. Unfortunately, most of us don't slow down long enough to find out what that truly is.

Instead, we've unknowingly picked up values, desires, and attitudes along the road of life, which are shaping the choices we make every day. How we invest our lives here on this earth is largely determined by these unseen motivations that are swirling within.

Most of us unconsciously watched our parents model a certain lifestyle – parts of which we adopted without even realizing it. What did your parents want in this life? Think for a moment about their approach to work. What did they do on the weekends? How did they spend the family's money? What seemed to be most important thing in their lives? Were your mother's desires different than your father's?

As you think about your family, what would you say that each one of them truly wanted in this life? What did your father long for? What was he willing to give up in order to get it? What about your mother? Where was her focus?

My guess is that some of those things resonate with you... and yet others don't.

Even if we find an internal reason to distance ourselves from their choices, more often than not we end up living a life that is profoundly informed by our home of origin. We end up taking a similar path and uttering many of the same parental words that we disdained as a kid.

As we start to develop a mind of our own through the influence of our education, peers, and even the media, we begin to make choices as to what our own desires will be. That's not only true about the clothes we wear, the classes we take, and the jobs we pursue...but it has to do with the entire trajectory of our lives.

Early on, my parents gave me the opportunity to experience and enjoy all sorts of activities – from academics to the arts to sports. Although they supported me in all my efforts, it was clear that my grades were most important of all. My dad pushed me to "do my best" which he seemed to assume involved straight A's. When I'd get a B from time to time, I was asked how I could increase it to an A. When I got an A on a test, I was jokingly asked if there was extra credit that I could have received as well.

The message that was being communicated was, "Outward performance is the key to a successful life."

Ironically, this meshed perfectly with my own internal wiring. Although I internally despised my dad's pushing, I rarely rebelled or fought against it. Instead, I worked even harder to get the A and simultaneously gain my dad's approval. It wasn't until mid-way through college that my resentment boiled to the surface, and we had a little 'chat' about my feelings on the subject.

In reality, my dad had very positive intentions by pushing me to excel. He wanted me to maximize the gifts and talents I was blessed with and ultimately be successful in life. He wished that his parents had expected more out of him. Instead of encouraging him to excel, his parents gave him a bit of slack when it came to grades and self-discipline.

Where You Are Is No Accident

In response to my dad's nudging, I kept pursuing success into adulthood. Toward the end of college, I saw an opportunity to pursue a Master's degree. My goal was to walk the graduation line twice in one day...receiving both my BA and MA within four years. During that last year of college, I got married, worked three part-time jobs, carried a huge load of units, and managed to stay somewhat sane. I accomplished my goal of crossing the stage twice that day, but I was so burned out that I never completed my Master's thesis. Instead, I transferred my units to another university a couple of years later and completed an even more extensive MA program.

As I made my way into my career at a non-profit, I started working more and more hours. Five years later, I founded a new non-profit and was working 70-80 hours a week...desperately wanting to see lives changed and the organization expand.

All of this was driven by what I wanted out of life.
Success.

I wanted people to see me as someone who made a significant impact. I wanted to bolster my identity with accomplishments so that I wouldn't feel the emptiness inside. I wanted to get an A, and I desperately wanted to be *somebody*.

Unfortunately, what I wanted drove me to complete burnout...resulting in a disconnected marriage and an affair.

You've got to know that I didn't ultimately land in a psych ward on accident. I spent three days under the supervision of doctors, because I made deliberate choices that were an unhealthy expression of my deepest desires. I landed there because of what I wanted and how I pursued it.

The truth is that you are where you are because of what you want out of this life. You were motivated in such a way to make decisions that have gotten you to this point in time.

Of course, there are some of us who have experienced abuse, tragedy, or hardship that was completely out of our control. I'm not insinuating that those things occurred in your life (or mine) because of decisions we directly made. Yet, in response to those experiences, we often take on a victim mentality, which handicaps us from moving forward with healthy intentions.

Whether you were abused, cheated on, fired unjustly, or wrongfully accused of something, the way you respond says a great deal about what you want in this life. You and I can embrace a view of ourselves that says, "I deserve the bad things that come my way"...or..."I shouldn't ever expect good things to happen to me"...or..."People can't be trusted, and they're always out to get me."

Ultimately, the things you focus on create the intentions that define the trajectory of your life. It is this trajectory that determines how you'll spend your time and what goals you'll set for yourself as well. My guess is that you'll start to discover what you currently want out of life as you reflect on these three questions.

1. What do you think and dream about?

Our minds are so powerful that what we focus upon has the ability to propel us toward that very focal point. In fact, you have a choice when you wake up. Will you focus on positive things that reinforce an anticipation of greatness to come? Or, will you extend your antenna searching for the negativity surrounding you?

As you go about your day, what do you meditate on? What do you turn over and over in your mind? Problems, potential solutions, or nothing at all?

Do you veg out every chance you get? Or, do you keep your mind active and engaged with people and projects?

What do you dream about for the future? Something that's connected to your life's passions? Or, a pipe dream (like winning the lottery) so you won't have to deal with your present reality?

2. What experiences do you exchange your time for?

Most of us spend the majority of our weekdays (8-12 hours) generating income through what is known as a job. Do you enjoy it? Is it aligned with your life passions and goals? Or, are you just waiting for the weekend to arrive?

After work, what do you choose to exchange your time for? Family? TV? Internet? Exercise? Creative activities?

On the weekends, think about how you fill those two days. Inside or outside? Alone or with people? Working, volunteering, relaxing?

3. What goals do you have for your life?

We all have goals, but most of us just don't take the time to write them down and make them explicit or connected to a timeline.

Instead, we usually have unstated, implicit goals that are rather nebulous or weak at best. Such as…"I'm just trying to survive"… or…"I want save some money for the future"…or…"I plan to start my own business"…or…"I want to be rich and famous without having to do anything."

As you think about your own life, what goals (stated or unstated) have you set for yourself?

By answering these questions honestly, you'll start to unearth what you've been wanting out of life. This isn't a case of right, wrong, good, or bad. What we really want may be different than what we're getting out of life right now.

After evaluating what you're experiencing right now in your life… do you *still* want the same thing? Probably not.

Because you've picked up this book, my guess is that there's something within you that's dissatisfied with what you're experiencing thus far. By choosing to want something different and setting your intentions in a new direction, you'll soon begin to see some very different results. Maybe it would be helpful to begin thinking about some shifts you'd like to make.

Choosing What You Want
As I called a friend from the pay phone in the narrow hallway of the psych ward, all I wanted was a few sheets of large white paper and a black marker. I was dying to post it on the white walls of my room and dream about the future. I knew what I wanted up until that point in time just wasn't working for me. I wanted something different, and I had to get it down in ink so that I could see it with clarity.

After I finally got my hands on the coveted paper, I taped it to wall and drew a thick line down the center. On the top left, I wrote "OLD LIFE" in giant letters…followed by "NEW LIFE" on the top right.

Over the course of two hours, that huge sheet of paper was filled up with my confession of the old life and a passionate desire for a new one.

In my old life, I was a driven workaholic who was consumed by my work at the non-profit. In my new life, I wanted to experience a passionate life with an ability to turn my drive on and off.

In my old life, I had a disconnected marriage and family life that was lived out of obligation. In my new life, I wanted a strong connection with my kids and an intimate marriage (which I assumed would not be my wife *or* the woman who just left me).

In my old life, I had a high need to control the outcomes. In my new life, I wanted to do my part and trust God with the rest.

As I looked over the entire list, there were several themes that began to emerge. It was clear that I wanted to begin making five transitions that I hoped would change the entire trajectory of my life.

- **From Anxious to Peaceful**
    I had a constant buzz in my brain, and I didn't even realize it. In

fact, I thought it was normal. I could be talking to you face to face, but my mind was going through a long list of things I needed to be doing that were more important.

In the days after I was released from the hospital, a friend suggested that I get a brain scan through the Amen Clinic in Newport Beach, California, and the process changed my life. The scan, which indicates levels of activity in the brain, showed that my basal ganglia was extremely over-active. This area of the brain responds to issues of 'fight or flight', and the overactivity was causing a low level of constant anxiety. Instead of responding in a socially awkward manner, I funneled it into working constantly. It felt like I could never shut down my brain. I longed for a peaceful mind...and life.

- **From Driven to Motivated**
  I tackled everything in my life with an 'all or nothing' attitude. And, usually, I gave it my all. This drivenness caused a disconnection in many of my relationships – especially in the case of my wife and kids. My ability to become ultra-focused was a huge asset in getting things done, but it was destroying my life as a whole.

  I wanted to experience a high level of motivation with the ability to turn the drive on and off. I started to wonder if it was possible to use this incredible gift that I was given without it causing so much relational fragmentation.

- **From Selling to Investing**
  Because of the leadership role that I held in the organization, I was constantly driving us forward toward growth and expansion. In many cases, that required me to sell the vision and sell people on leveraging their resources to be part of the next step. Despite the fact that the goals of the organization were good in and of themselves, I ended up using people to fuel the growth rather than investing in them and allowing the expansion to happen naturally.

  I was tired of selling people on a vision. I was weighed down by the fact that I was burning people out when the mission of the organization was supposed to be for their own benefit. I wanted to be investing in people rather than building an institution...I just wasn't sure how to do it.

- **From Isolation to Intimacy**
  Because of my overworking, I found myself more and more isolated from authentic relationships. My head was buried in projects more than it was open to people. I'm a self-starter who works well alone, but I can get lost in my own grand ideas. I can also end up running over people that get in my way when I lack sensitivity to their perspective or emotions.

  More than anything, I wanted intimacy. That's the whole reason why I left my wife to begin with...to develop an intimate, loving relationship with another woman. I wanted a great marriage, and I longed for close friendships with people who I didn't have to lead or sell a vision to.

- **From Momentum to In The Moment**
  I had been living for momentum. Everything in my life centered on how to be effective, efficient, and productive in order to gain the 'Big Mo' as I liked to call it. Specifically, this was true about my work-life within the non-profit organization I founded. Unfortunately, that desire for momentum was taking me out of the moment.

  When a staff member or volunteer leader had an issue or a struggle, I had a difficult time being present for them. Instead, I was concerned about how it was going to negatively impact the organization. My head was already brainstorming all the ways that I could 'grease the rails' so that nothing would slow down or lose momentum. Yet, I was constantly tired.

  Frankly, I didn't want to push anymore. I wanted to take it easy... even though I felt guilty. I longed for the day when I could look someone in the eye (especially my wife and kids) and not be

What Do I Want?

thinking about anything else. I just wanted to be present and in the moment...not consumed by the momentum of my life or an organization.

After asking myself "Who am I?", the second question that I needed to ask was "What do I want?" As I continued to discover my identity, I simultaneously was unearthing my true desires for this life.

Until that point, I had fallen into the rut of unseen motivations that were more base or raw...longing for nebulous success in order to soothe that place within me that was hurting and broken. Now, at rock bottom, I was re-evaluating everything including my own aspirations.

I will admit that asking "What do I want?" can quickly lead me to answering with a long list of to-dos. That's simply because 'doing' was my chosen path to getting that proverbial A in life. This is the reason why I chose to continually ask a question of inner desire rather than outward goals.

The action steps will come later, but first you must determine the very essence of what you desire in this life. In those moments in my hospital room, I was finally able to come to a place to say my true desires were...

> Peace
> Motivation
> Investment in others
> Intimate relationships
> Living in the moment

When I find myself at 99 years old surrounded by my children and grandchildren, I want to look back on the days of my life and be able to see evidence of that kind of life. If I gaze into my 40s, 50s, and 60s and see successful companies that I've built yet I haven't been at peace, I doubt I'll be satisfied. If I become famous and wealthy yet I've been driven and disconnected from intimate relationships, I can't imagine I'll be happy with the course of my life.

So...*what do you want?*

This is the broad brush stroke of your life. It's not the fine details of goals and timelines and budgets. This is the overarching theme of the story of your life.

It's your life's trajectory.

In the months after my hospital visit, I continued to re-align my own trajectory. I was refining what I wanted out of life on a daily basis. As I spent time with my kids, I'd ask myself, "How do my thoughts and actions align with what I truly want in this life?"

If I say that I want an intimate relationship with my kids, why would I be texting or talking on the phone or looking at Twitter while I'm with them? It's incongruent with what I truly want.

If I say that I want to be peaceful and motivated, why would I think of structuring a new business or non-profit in a way that would provoke anxiety and stimulate a desire to be driven and overwork? That wouldn't align with the new trajectory for my life.

So often, we're more concerned about our day-to-day task list, immediate desires, and momentary troubles that it's almost inconceivable for us to take the time to reflect deeply upon our life's course.

Are you getting the results you want?

If not, now is the time to do something about it. Don't waste another day heading in a direction that you don't even want to be going. Slam on the brakes of your life and start asking yourself some tough questions.

If you're wondering how and when to do it...

1. Set aside specific time to reflect.
Don't expect significant breakthroughs to occur on your commute to and from work. You need to set aside measurable time to quiet

your soul and ask yourself some tough questions. My life melted down, and I checked into a hospital to stabilize myself. It was in the midst of that quietness that reflection was possible. I'd encourage you to put on the brakes before you get to that point.

Take a weekend road trip...or take a day off work...or at least carve out an entire Saturday morning. Whatever it takes...just get alone and take some time to ask questions and reflect. This won't be the time when all the answers are mystically downloaded into your brain. It's simply a marker in time to get started with the process.

2. Ask God to give you direction.
If God created me, I have a hunch that God has a good idea what's best for me as well. Therefore, when I'm looking for input when it comes to the direction of my life, asking for a Nudge is one of the first things that I do.

In my faith, Jesus teaches that if we ask for something, God won't give us an evil or harmful gift. He challenges us to seek and knock...the promised results are an open door. It's amazing how things will begin to align when I'm willing to open myself up to the One who created me. You may want to try it as well.

3. Make your own "old life / new life" list.
Buy a giant poster board or snag a big sheet of paper from the conference room at the office. Put a line down the middle and start listing things in your 'old life' that are dragging you down. List corresponding 'new life' experiences in the other column. Don't worry about it all being perfect or set in stone. This is all a rough draft. It's just the beginning of the process of re-launching your life.

What you're doing is looking back at the path you've been on and looking ahead toward a new path. Just because you've lived a certain way until this point in time doesn't mean that you have to keep living that way.

You have the power to re-launch your life, and asking what you want is a powerful step that can't be skipped. Clarifying your deepest desires will help you stay on course on those days when it would be much easier to just give in to whatever is most convenient.

Living a lifestyle of convenience rarely gives anyone a rich and meaningful life.

What Truths Will Keep Me Focused?

chapter 06

As we continue setting the trajectory of our lives, we'll need truths to keep us focused and prevent us from straying off course. Unfortunately as we go throughout each day, we're bombarded with thoughts and conversations that cause us to believe negative things about ourselves, other people, and even the world at large.

There are forces of good and evil which are at odds for our hearts, minds, and devotion. Much of this is happening underneath the surface in what is called the unconscious (or spiritual) realm. Just because you can't see it doesn't mean that it isn't real or that it isn't happening.

In other cultures around the world, it is *assumed* that these forces are at work while much of Western culture writes it off as merely hocus-pocus. I have come to believe that there is a darkness that seeks to eradicate that which is beautiful and life-giving within us. Whether or not you put a name or face on this 'dark voice' is up to you, but it serves us well to open the eyes of our hearts to that which isn't seen with the naked eye.

We have been designed to have a full life which is built upon the foundation of our identity. Meanwhile dark forces are seeking to undermine this truth. He/she/it knows that if we are willing to believe something other than the truth of our divine imprint, wiring, and strengths, our lives will be much less than they were intended to be. The greatest tactic to undermine the truth is through the weapon of 'lies.'

In reality, these lies speak to our deepest insecurities. They come from voices that speak bold promises…seeking to seduce us away from who we are and what we truly want in this life. The lies try to get us to prove we are worth something. They suggest that we won't be loved unless we're successful, beautiful, and powerful. These lies cause us to question our own self-worth and turn to other things to find some momentary sense of fulfillment.

These lies don't live on the surface. No…they plunge deep into the inner recesses of our soul to find those places where cracks and brokenness can be found. They wedge their way in and seek to create a fragmenting of our identity…resulting in a never-ending need to prove ourselves to people around us.

The dark voice challenges the truth that each one of us is uniquely created with strengths, talent, and beauty…and that we're loved wholeheartedly by the One who created us.

Life vs. Death
The ultimate result of these lies is our death…not necessarily our physical demise but our spiritual and relational destruction. Truths, on the other hand, are a source of life. It's helpful to look closely at the results of believing one or the other. See if this resonates with you…

- **Lies steal your hope for the future. Truths re-affirm there is an amazing plan and purpose for your life.**

    The way you envision the future of your life will largely determine its outcome. If you believe the lie that you have no future and that it's destined to be bleak, you'll probably find a way to make it that way. Yet, if you choose to believe the truth that your life (and future) has meaning, you will discover a rich life that's in store for you.

- **Lies kill your authentic relationships. Truths give you confidence to connect intimately with others.**

    The truth is that you were created for relationship. You were designed to connect intimately with other human beings...sharing experiences, hopes, dreams, frustrations, and failures with one another. If you believe the lie that others can't be trusted or that no one wants to be with you, you'll experience lonely isolation... even if you're constantly surrounded by other human beings. Confidence comes from believing the truth about who you are.

- **Lies destroy the foundation of your life...your identity. Truths reinforce your identity.**

    Your identity is the most important part of your life. Without a strong foundation, you'll be compensating continually for the lack of strength. If you believe the lie that you're worth less than others, you'll be out to prove your self-worth every chance you get. If you don't embrace that others love you, you'll do anything you can to get people to display their love. In the process, your true identity will slowly erode, and you'll find yourself with nothing more than a façade for a life. Yet, if you believe the truth about who you are and who you have been created to be, you'll find life...a rich and meaningful life!

The question isn't whether or not you'll hear lies.
The question is...what will you do when you hear them?

Although negative thoughts can arise without external stimuli, most lies are triggered by something you hear someone else say to you or about you.

For instance, your spouse may say something like, *"I wish you would listen to what I say."* When you hear this, it's easy to respond by believing a lie, such as, *"I never do it right,"* or *"I'm not a good husband or wife."*

Oftentimes, we don't even realize that this negative thought – this lie – is swirling around in our minds and hearts until it's adversely affected our day...and our relationships. The lie we've believed may put us in a mild funk all day or it may completely unravel us to the point of tears. If left to its own devices, the lie will seek to erode our identity and ultimately our effectiveness in life, work, and relationships.

Some lies are hard *not* to believe, especially those that have followed us from childhood. Early lies such as *"There's something wrong with me"* or *"I'm not good enough"* take root deep within us and shape the adult we become.

Lies often include words that reveal an unrealistic expectation or comparison...

- *"There's something wrong with you."*
- *"You're not good enough."*
- *"You're not pretty enough."*
- *"You're not as smart as your brother."*
- *"You're just like your father."*

When we begin to recognize statements like these as lies, we can combat them by returning our focus to the truth.

What Is The Truth?
If we've believed a lie about ourselves long enough, the truth can actually sound like a lie. It requires someone outside of our family dynamic and life situation to help us see the truths of life.

Take a moment and read the list of common lies with the corresponding truths. Start by saying, "The lie is..." as you read from column one. Then, look at the second column and say, "But the truth is..." Some of these may not be an issue for you, but there are probably at least a few that you struggle with from time to time.

LIES	TRUTHS
I'm not good enough	I am created with a divine imprint, and I am remarkable.
People don't love me or want to be with me.	Even if my parents were unable to love me, every person is loved by God.
I'm not attractive.	I am very attractive, because I was created by God.
I need to be perfect to be loved, feel good, and be accepted.	I need to accept myself and others for who we are – with both strengths and weaknesses.
I'm not athletic / smart / talented.	I am athletic, smart, and talented in my own unique way.
I deserve to be belittled and abused.	No one deserves abuse of any kind – physical or emotional.
I'm so bad I can't be forgiven.	Nothing is beyond forgiveness.
If I perform perfectly, I will be loved.	Love has nothing to do with perfection…it is a gift.
I should keep my struggles a secret.	Healing comes through honesty and authenticity with those we love.
I am prideful or conceited if I like myself and the gifts and talents I've been given.	A strong foundation is built as I embrace who I have been created to be.

Out of the 10 lies that are listed, which ones most resonate with you? Can you see how they can play out in your life on a daily basis? In all practicality, these lies aren't confined to the dark recesses of your mind. They dramatically impact the way that you think about the world, how you interact with co-workers, and the degree to which you are able to love and be loved.

Lies and truths determine the trajectory of your life.

Believing the lies about yourself simply sucks the life out of your relationships. Yet, when you're willing to do the work of identifying the lie and applying the truth of who you truly are, your confidence increases and your relationships improve.

The beauty of a life launch is that it transforms us from the inside out. It's not about trying to help you get rich or lose weight or save your marriage. It's about helping you build a new foundation for your life – a foundation that's solid to launch from. Your identity can be found in these rich truths – not in what others say about you – and not even in what you say about yourself.

Your identity is found in who the Creator of the universe created you to be. In fact, who knows you better than the One who created you?

The amazing thing is that our behaviors and relationships start to change as we embrace this truth. We start to feel better about ourselves, and we start to behave in new ways. This positive change simply flows out of who we are at the deepest place within us.

Did you notice that you started feeling a bit better about yourself and about life as you were trying on these truths? The more you embrace this truth-filled identity…the stronger your foundation will be in the process of launching your life.

Step Into the Courtroom of Your Mind

In order to combat these lies, we have the opportunity to step into the courtroom of our minds and defend ourselves. We must come with a briefcase full of evidence – ready to provide full documentation of the truth.

Are you ready to try this on?

Think of a negative experience that you had recently. Perhaps you had a run-in with your spouse before work, and you felt down all day long. Or, maybe your boss corrected you for something you did, and you just couldn't shake it. Whatever the experience was, run it through this process, and I'll share one of mine with you as well.

1. Identify the lie clearly.

If you're feeling down or just plain funky, you can rest assured that you're believing a lie about something. If you allow that feeling to remain nebulous and unclear, it will slowly eat you from the inside out. To combat the lie (and ultimately defeat it), you'll need to get clear on exactly what lie you're choosing to believe in that moment.

In the months (and even years) prior to leaving my wife for another woman, I was extremely disenchanted with our marriage. I was so focused on my work at the non-profit, and my wife was consumed as the primary parent of our children and her teaching job. We had become more like roommates than anything else... very little fighting, but very little connection. The lie I believed was, "My wife can never be the partner in life and marriage that I truly desire...another woman will satisfy that deep-down craving I have." Unfortunately, I wasn't able to see this as a lie until it was way too late.

2. Determine the corresponding truth.

Once we clearly articulate the lie, we're able to then find a corresponding truth. You may want to refer back to the list of 10 commonly believed lies that we addressed a few moments ago. Do you find your lie listed there? If so, what is the truth that stands in opposition?

If you don't see your lie on that list, what belief can you embrace that provides life rather than death? Remember that a lie leads to death while truth leads to life. If you can't come up with a truth immediately, head down the road toward that which will bring you lasting life...and you'll find the truth you need to embrace.

In my case, I believed the lie that "My wife could never be the partner I needed and wanted." In reality, this false belief is more about me and my inability to be the partner she needed me to be.

I discovered that I needed to initiate the type of relationship I desired and bring that partnership to the table *myself*.

The truth is…"I can develop a great marriage and partnership as I'm willing to serve my wife and family with the love that I ultimately desire."

3. Back up the truth with solid evidence.
Stating the truth in the courtroom of your mind is powerful, but backing it up with evidence is essential. When you walk in, it is best to be armed with a briefcase full of corroborating testimony to draw upon - real-life experiences, previous positive conversations, and other tangible verification. Believe me when I say…the dark voices will stand up to you with plenty of evidence to support the lie.

"David, your wife doesn't even care about you. She's not passionate about you, she's not interested in your work, and she spends all her time with the kids. You're not a priority in her life."

That was the so-called 'evidence' I would hear in my head prior to leaving to be with her best friend. Ironically, this was probably more projection on my part than anything else. There was more evidence that these things were true about me rather than her. In the process of me setting the trajectory of my heart back toward her, would I believe the lies flowing from the dark voices, or would I find the truth and present life-giving evidence?

Because I had a sense that restoring my marriage was ultimately the best thing for my life and family, I sought out my own evidence.

I intentionally focused on how my wife had sacrificed so much for our children and me over our 14 years of marriage. I remembered how she supported me in all my vocational adventures and how she put up with my hilarious antics that wouldn't have been acceptable in the eyes of most wives. This sacrifice and support on her part showed that she cares deeply about me and that she has loved me faithfully. This evidence fueled my effort to not only re-launch my life...but to re-launch our relationship.

4. Anticipate a positive outcome.

It is virtually impossible to believe a lie and anticipate a positive outcome in your life situation. The very essence of a lie is that it is a withdrawal from life. It sucks out the marrow...the goodness... the beauty. Believing the lie only results in a negative viewpoint.

You may say, "Well, I'm not a negative person! I think positively about life...I just don't think we'll ever be friends though."

You're right. If you believe that you won't be friends, you probably won't be. And, you may think that you're a positive person, but the lies that you're believing about that person (and yourself) aren't limited to that particular relationship. The lies will slowly erode the foundation of your life...rendering you unstable and weak in all your relationships.

As I was living alone...30 minutes away from my family, the positive outcome that I envisioned was the restoration of my marriage. I began to imagine opportunities when I could appropriately care for my wife as she was ready. Although I committed to allow her to take her time and initiate every step of reconnection, I made it clear with my thoughts and words that I was ready, willing, and able to work on our relationship.

I wasn't sure if she would ever be willing to take me back, but I was focused on the possibility of a positive outcome.

In your particular situation...the situation where you've believed the lie...what would be a positive outcome?

Can you envision a restored relationship? Could you imagine your health being transformed? Might you be able to see a new job that's a great fit for your skills, talents, and experience?

The Discipline of Believing the Truth

Our minds have been beautifully crafted with the ability to process great amounts of data…and wander all over the place. It's amazing how the smallest thing can send my mind down a rabbit trail of evidence that will ultimately lead to death.

When I'm hungry, angry, lonely, or tired, the lies that find their way into my mind seem intensely believable. The dark voices come up with elaborate evidence to present the lie in a way that is both possible and inviting. It's as though no other options even exist.

> *"You'll never find and enjoy your purpose in life."*
>
> Crap, that is so true. I've been searching for years trying to figure out what to do with my life.
>
> *"Your wife is tired of waiting around for you to figure it out."*
>
> She's tired of hearing me complain about being bored or tired or frustrated. She probably wishes I would just get an ordinary 9-5 job like all the other husbands.
>
> *"You want to make a difference in this world, but you don't even know where to begin."*
>
> I am such a *loser*. I'm almost 40, and I haven't made it yet.

See how that works? These may not be your lies, but don't act as if you don't have any. There are things you believe about yourself on a daily basis that are holding you back from experiencing the life you've always wanted. If you don't identify the handful of lies that are holding you back, you'll miss out on the life launch you're preparing for.

Are you willing to be disciplined in the way you think? When you're in a funk, are you prepared to slow down your thinking to determine what lie you've been believing? Are you ready to find the truth and back it up with evidence?

This way of thinking and living requires discipline.

It's easy to allow our minds to run amok and head down a dark trail littered with lies that taste like candy fresh out of the wrapper and end up poisoning our very souls.

Stop and think.
Identify the lie, and apply the truth.
Anticipate the positive.
Life will be different.

How Will I Take Action?

chapter 07

Have you ever come across someone who is constantly talking about the great things they're going to do in life? This is the person that always has a great idea, but it never quite seems to come to fruition. The next time you see them...they're already onto the next thing. They jump from project to project without getting the traction needed in order to take action.

The traction they need is a strategic action plan.
That's what you're ready for.

Now is the time to build on all the work we've been doing up until this point and begin to develop a strategic plan that will get you going. If you get stuck with all the reflecting and never take action, you're not experiencing a life launch...you're just stuck on the launch pad in the same situation you've always been in. Even if the action is a bit off-course, at least you're moving and you can correct your trajectory along the way.

Remember the launch pad you're developing and how it is providing you with the new trajectory for your life...

1. Your foundation is your identity.
If you are unclear on your identity, you'll struggle with your life every single day. You'll be wondering who you are, and you'll look to an unending stream of people and things to tell you. You'll try to please other people, because they will want you to be someone you're not. Get clear on who you are, and your foundation will be solid. You'll continue to discover new things about yourself as you grow and develop, but the clarity of your identity will create a firm footing to launch from.

2. Your eyes are set on what you want in this life.
The fogginess of life is lifting as you ask, "What do I want?" You may be very clear on exact aspects of your life…whether it's your health, job, or friendships. Or, you may be more like me…focused on the type of life you want rather than the exact details.

This image will become more clear in the next few minutes as we develop a mental picture of your preferable future…your vision.

3. You are replacing the lies with the truth.
The dark voice is no longer nebulous chatter that is indistinguishable from reality within your mind. You are getting clear on the lies you've believed, and the truth stands in contrast. As you 'try on' the truth, it feels a bit awkward, but you're feeling the difference. You're moving from darkness to light. You're seeing the possibilities, and you're feeling hope for the first time in areas of your life where you gave up some time ago.

In chapter 3, which is entitled "What If…?", I started to ask questions to open up new possibilities in your life. Although that was a good start, you're now ready to get serious about envisioning the future. Allow your mind and heart to be wide open to where Wisdom will lead you. Don't limit the possibilities, and don't worry about all the details quite yet.

Your Vision
Your vision is one of the most captivating things about your life. While your identity gives you a strong foundation, your vision is the fuel that

empowers you to re-launch. This mental picture of your preferable future is what gives you the strength to pull yourself out of bed on those days that seem bleak.

Without a vision, you'll find yourself in the rut of life…probably a rut that you learned from your parents as you grew up. It's that 'default' place that you go to when nothing else seems captivating or motivating.

Don't settle for the default groove of life. Be courageous enough to close your eyes and open up your heart to see what you really want. I believe in you, and I'm standing with you in this courageous process. You are not alone.

Although we'll look at each of The Seven Spheres of Transformation in the third section of this book, I want you to get a broad vision for your life right now.

One year from now, *what do you envision for your life?*

Close your eyes and ask yourself. What do you see? Is your family surrounding you? What about friends? Are you enjoying your job/vocation/passions? What about your income? Is it enough? More than enough? Are you generous?

What about your health? And your love life? Your spirituality?

Where are you living? What is surrounding you in your home? What colors do you see? Do you know your neighbors? What experiences are important to you?

What emotions are you feeling as you envision this new life?

Lock in that mental picture. This is the vision of your life, and it is important. It is sacred, and you should treat it that way. Capture the scene that embodies the type of life you want to be living. Allow the sights, sounds, smells, and emotions to envelope you. These things will provoke you to take action to experience this preferable future.

When I close my eyes, let me tell you what I see.

I see a confident man with his head held high and his feet firmly planted on the ground. I see his heart pounding with passion and compassion, and his arms are extended to the right and the left. They're surrounding his wife and family who are constantly growing and being transformed.

His entire family is traveling throughout the United States and even the world from time to time as they share their strength and hope with others. This man is leading the way as the chief servant of his family, and he's investing in others through the gifts, talents, and experiences that he's been given. He's writing books and resources, and he speaks to gatherings of people – hundreds, thousands, and tens of thousands about a rich, meaningful life…about marriage, compassionate work, and spirituality.

Thousands of people around the globe are benefiting from his work.

His financial needs are met, and he's not pushing for more. He is enjoying every minute of life. His marriage is intimate. His family is connected. His soul is full and overflowing, and I see a smile on his face.

This man is me. This is the vision that comes to my mind when I close my eyes. What do you see for your own life?

Your Values
Your values are principles that embody what's most important to you as an individual. These have been shaped over time through your culture, family of origin, spirituality, life experiences, and personal choices. Most of us are not inherently aware of our values on a daily basis, but they determine the choices we make moment by moment.

These life principles determine how you spend your time and money. They guide the decisions you make about where you live, who you marry, and how you'll raise your kids. *Everything is shaped by your values.*

The more aware you are of what's important to you…the greater the opportunity you have to ensure that you continually align your life with those values.

1. **What 3-6 values do you see embedded within your vision?**
   As you think about the mental picture of your preferable future, what values seem to be essential to that moment? Take each aspect of the snapshot in your mind's eye and seek to understand the underlying principle that is derived from that scene.

   Within my vision, I see several values emerge. The man in that moment (me) values a strong sense of identity. He is confident in how God has uniquely wired him – with both strengths and weaknesses. Therefore, self-awareness and acceptance is a high value.

   I also see a value for intimate relationships…particularly with his family. His family is with him, and they are joining in the journey of life. He isn't off doing his own thing all alone. They are a connected family unit, and he is serving them along the way.

   Finally, I notice a strong value for life-change. Not only does he want to continue being transformed, but he wants to share his learnings, experiences, and life with those who are in need of life-change as well. There is a great sense of generosity in his willingness to open up the innermost part of his life for the sake of others.

2. **As you think about each value, what does it mean to you?**
   Defining the value is essential, but so is reflecting on the nature of it as well. Perhaps you'd like to take out several sheets of paper… equal to the number of values that you defined. Write the name of the value in the center of the page, and then begin to describe the value in the surrounding space.

   I would pull out three pieces of paper and write the following words in the center…strong identity, intimate relationships, and life-change. I would take some time to elaborate on each of them. For instance, on the paper that says "strong identity," I write…

- Someone who is confident in who they are.
- Accepting both their strengths and weaknesses.
- Not blown to and fro by the winds of life.
- Doesn't want to be driven by a need to 'succeed' anymore.
- Less worried about the opinions of others and more focused on his vision.

These descriptions help me hone in on what's really important about that value in my life. The more I understand why I value that…the more likely I'll embrace it even more. This will ensure that I stay on track to ultimately experience my vision come to fruition.

3. What does each value call you to do in your life now?
If something is truly important to you, it will call you to take action. As you reflect on the importance of each value in your life, my guess is that one of two things will happen.

If you see that your life is *not* embodying that value at the present time, you'll probably hear a Voice calling you to make some value-aligning decisions in the near future. If you see that intimate relationships are important within the framework of your vision but you don't invest much time in them now, you'll probably feel called to change how you spend your time. If you envision a desire to make a positive impact on the world around you but you notice that most of your time is spent on yourself, you may feel called to adjust your focus.

On the other hand, you may be living out that value in a beautiful way already…but you're feeling called to take it up a notch. Perhaps you've become somewhat complacent. Maybe you'd like to stretch yourself and experience that value in a whole new way. How each value calls us to take action is deeply personal, and only you will know what steps to take.

Your Strategy
Your strategy is a launch plan that will guide you on your journey for

the next year. Without a strategy and a plan, all this launch-talk is just that…talk. You need to take practical steps each and every day in order to see your life transformed into the mental picture you envisioned a few minutes ago.

I find that envisioning a compelling, long-range mental picture combined with a practical, strategic plan empowers me to do things that I didn't even think were possible for my life. Let's plan our lives, and live our plans.

1. What goals would you like to set with a one-year timeline?
One year may seem like a long time in your mind, but I believe that it is a solid time frame that allows for great progress and some grace as well. The first goal that comes to mind may be where you are in the most pain or where you long to see the most progress.

For instance, you may want to re-launch your physical health and be 25 pounds lighter in the next year. Maybe you want to start your own business and transition out of your current job. Or, perhaps you want to go back to college and earn your degree.

My guess is that you'll want to set a goal in each one of The Seven Spheres of Transformation when we look at them in the third section of this book. For now though, I'd encourage you to come up with 2-3 goals that are most important to you.

Grab a sheet of paper, and write them down as specific statements. "Within one year, I will _____."

2. What are your strategic next steps for each goal?
You have the mental picture of your preferable future.
You're clear on what you value.
You've set 2-3 goals for the next year.
What is it going to take to get there?
What are you going to do about it?

For every goal, make a list of all the action steps needed in order to see it come to fruition. At some point, you may not be able to see far enough into the future or understand all the variables, but go as far as you can.

After our reconciliation, my family and I set a goal a couple of years ago to open a children's home in southern India. I had already travelled to the area 6-7 times in previous years, and we had a close relationship with an organization called "Harvest India." I saw a need for a home in the slums of Chennai, and Harvest India was willing to be the hands and feet if we could rally financial supporters.

We envisioned the future and developed an action plan. Step by step, we lived out the plan. We started a non-profit. We launched a website. We rallied monthly supporters. We gave the thumbs up, and Harvest India opened the home.

After saving up our own family finances, our family of four travelled to Chennai during a two week Christmas break to dedicate the home and visit the beautiful children. What an amazing experience!

Do you think it would have been possible without a vision? How about without a solid strategic plan?

Admittedly, I am deeply passionate about vision, values, goals, and strategy. There is something about envisioning the future and discovering why I'm passionate about that mental picture that is invigorating. I think it's because I love to experience positive change and have the privilege of seeing others receive the benefits in their own lives.

You Have the Capacity
So many people believe the lie that things can never change. It's just not true. You have the capacity to re-launch your life in a different direction. I believe that the Creator has fashioned you in such a way that you have the power to create a new path with an unending supply of resources at your disposal.

How Will I Take Action?

If you want the resources, they are available to you. All you have to do is reach out to receive them. Ignore the dark voices and begin to assemble a scaffolding of truth. Climb up on it, and begin constructing a new life piece by piece.

Lay out the map of the universe and realize that the edges of the page no longer exist. You have been empowered to travel beyond where you've ever imagined. Envision an adventurous path with a new destination.

If you want to...

- Engage your life passions, I'm telling you that you can.
- Enjoy an amazing romantic marriage, it is possible.
- Develop intimate friendships, you have the ability.
- Re-discover your own creativity and playfulness, you can do it.
- Enhance your physical well-being, you have the power.
- Experience spirituality at a deeper level, you will.

Do you believe that these things are true?

If you don't believe that a life launch is possible for you, then you'll never experience one. Maybe you've lost all hope in a particular area of your life that you just can't even muster an ounce of faith.

Then, I'll lend you some of mine.

I have full belief and trust that you can experience tremendous life change if you're willing to take one step at a time each and every day. You don't have to accomplish everything all at once.

By looking into the future, you'll keep your eyes up and focused on what you want. By holding onto your values, you'll be able to steer your life in the right direction. By developing a strategic action plan, you'll ensure that every day is utilized to propel yourself toward your goals.

Your vision is possible if you're willing to take action.

Who Will Walk With Me?
chapter 08

In the days leading up to my life implosion, I was overwhelmed with more thoughts and emotions than I had ever experienced in my life.

I was completely disenchanted with my marriage, but I held a deep belief that an affair and divorce was morally wrong. I was tired of leading the non-profit I founded, but I felt utterly obligated to keep living out the vision I had cast to a growing constituency. I was passionately 'in love' with another woman, but she was my wife's best friend.

Because of my own personality and leadership style within the organization, I was rather isolated and lonely. I was seen as an authority figure, and I didn't share my innermost world with many people.

That's a recipe for disaster if you've ever seen one!

With all this swirling inside me, I couldn't keep it to myself, and I didn't feel comfortable going to my leadership team nor my wife…for obvious reasons. I felt stuck and all alone.

As I racked my brain for a source of help during this time, there were two people that I had a sneaking suspicion would be willing to help me…a friend who had walked through the same thing and a therapist I hadn't seen in over 10 years.

I started by calling my friend and letting him in on the state of my life, and he wasn't shocked. First of all, he knew the pace of life and leadership that I was running, and he assumed it couldn't last forever. Something has to give at some point in time. Secondly, he wasn't surprised, because he knows how fragile the human heart and life is. He knows that most everyone will 'break' in some way at some point in time, and restoration will be needed.

I talked. I cried. I cursed.
He listened. He empathized. He encouraged.
He committed to walking with me through the process.

My second call was to the therapist. My wife and I met him almost 20 years back at college where he was the head of the counseling center. We went to him for our pre-marital counseling, and he was part of our wedding ceremony. He meant a great deal to both of us, but I hadn't seen him in years. What I did know was that he was a wise man and that he cared about me as an individual, leader, husband, and father. After verifying that everything was confidential, I spilled my guts to him at our first meeting together.

I talked. I cried. I cursed.
He listened. He empathized. He encouraged.
He committed to walking with me through the process.

Do you see a pattern?

After two weeks, I pulled the trigger. I left my wife, and I resigned from the non-profit. I immediately moved into an apartment with the other woman, and a new life began. I re-launched my life…and I lost almost every 'friend' I had.

Because of my leadership role within this organization, let's just say that people were less than understanding with my decision. I received hate email, blog attacks, taunting in front of my home, and even word-of-mouth physical threats. People that I had spent the previous five years investing in were turning on me, but I was committed to this new life I had set out to create.

Despite all the hatred from others (fueled out of their own disappointment and pain), my therapist and friend stuck by my side...willing to walk with me through hell and back. In fact, two other friends joined with me for a six-month season that was unbelievably transformative. Three friends and a therapist...that's all I had.

Life Is Lonely Without Friends
The truth is that we were created to be relational beings. Relationships are part of the fabric of our lives, and when we we're lacking in that area, it's devastating. It may not feel immediately devastating on the surface...it's more like a slow fragmentation of one's inner world. It's an ache that resides deep in your gut...an ache of loneliness. It's a longing to be connected and supported and intimate.

If you don't have close friendships, you know that feeling.

Sure, you may hang out with people on a regular basis, but do you share you inner world with them? Do they know your hopes and dreams and aspirations? Can you call them in the middle of the night just to talk when your teenager isn't home yet? And, here's the big one...are they willing to help you move from one home to another?

Our culture is becoming more disconnected than ever before. We live in gated communities with seven-foot high fences separating our yards and patios. Most of us spend our time indoors as we're entertained by an endless stream of TV shows, movies, and websites. If we do venture outdoors, it's within the confines of our enclosed backyard where neighbors can't peer in to see us. Most of us don't even know our neighbors well enough to borrow an ingredient we're missing.

The John Wayne persona of rugged individualism has become pervasive to the point that we actually believe that we don't need other people. We celebrate lives that are lived without the assistance of others. We give accolades to those who pull themselves up by their own bootstraps to make it in this life.

In reality, we're missing out on one of the most precious gifts that human beings have to offer...relationships.

There is absolutely no way that I could have ever made it through my life implosion without those three friends and my therapist. Their friendship, support, and encouragement were (and are) priceless.

It Takes One to Know One
Their willingness to walk with me was a conscious decision on their part. It was an intentional choice to be with me during a season of life when I was completely alone. Although we were connected at one level prior to all of this, our hearts are intertwined now.

If you want that type of friend, it takes one to know one.

Rather than waiting for someone else to step up and be your friend, I want to challenge you to go first. Be courageous and start being the kind of friend you want in your own life. Don't be surprised when people don't immediately reciprocate with love and affection. Friendship, at the level I'm talking about, takes time to develop.

As I've mentioned before, a healthy individual usually has 1-3 very intimate friends, a circle of 10-20 ongoing friendships, 20-75 meaningful connections, and an unlimited amount of acquaintances.

We throw that word 'friend' around quite haphazardly. When most of us use it, we're referring to someone we see from time to time and have some level of pleasant interaction with. In other words, the person isn't someone we dislike.

In our culture, we don't really have another term to describe those who are willing to walk closely alongside us. When we're young, we may call someone our 'best friend', but that term isn't used much as an adult... especially among guys.

Maybe we should call them a launch-friend or mo-betta-friend or the friend-who's-willing-to-walk-with-me-when-I'm-an-ass. Not sure about that one. Anyway, I am sure that I need to be a true friend if I ever expect someone to be that type of friend to me.

1. A true friend reminds you of your identity.

I have enough people in my life that remind me of all my false starts and failed attempts and utterly tragic decisions. I need people who see me through the lens of my true identity. That's how I want to see people as well.

If I recognize the divine imprint within myself, I'll start to see that within others, too. Because they have been created with such a high level of value, I will value them with my words and actions. I'll treat them like the precious work of art that they truly are.

As a true friend, I'll remind them of their strengths when they're focusing on their weaknesses. I can encourage them to build on where they're already strong, and I won't give in to the temptation to magnify where they're deficient.

Rather than being put off by their distinct wiring (i.e., personality), I will celebrate their uniqueness. Their individuality is a strength in our relationship...allowing me to view the world in a different way.

I will treat their life story as sacred. I won't be flippant about the challenging experiences that my friend has walked through, and I will honor their heritage.

2. A true friend affirms your positive intentions.

When it comes to what you want in this life, I believe that you have positive intentions. It's rare that I find anyone who doesn't have an intention that's ultimately positive when they're seeking to take fresh steps in their life.

Even in the process of leaving my wife and leadership role, my positive intention was to develop an intimate relationship and find freedom and joy in my life. Unfortunately, the methods that I utilized were a bit flawed, but my intention was positive.

As a true friend, you have the opportunity to cheer people on as they express their positive intentions. You may not agree with everything they're doing and you may not even see the possibility of it all coming together, but you can affirm their intentions.

We are transformed most powerfully by walking through an experience and encountering some level of challenge and even pain. Thinking that you can prevent your friend from experiencing this is naïve and even unfruitful. By walking with them through the process, you'll be able to see their intentions fleshed out through the rough spots and ultimately through the re-launching of their life.

3. A true friend reinforces the truth in your life...not the lies.
The lies are so prominent in our lives that we don't need someone else reinforcing them. We don't need to be surrounded by other people who are believing the same lies, nor do we need people to undermine the truth.

Have you ever had a friend who said...?

- *"Don't even think about it...you'd get crushed."*
- *"I don't think you're cut out for that."*
- *"You can't do that...you're not _____ enough."*

Don't listen to them! In fact, you may consider losing them as a friend. You need to be surrounded by people (especially during the process of a life launch) who are reminding you of your greatness.

Look for friends who are more apt to say...

- *"You have been uniquely created by God."*
- *"Your personality is a gift to others."*

- *"Your strengths make me stronger."*
- *"I believe in you!"*

Ironically, the primary way that you can reinforce the truth in the lives of others is by embracing it in your own life. If you don't believe the truth about who you are and the great things that you're called to do, it's hard to invest that in other people.

4. A true friend challenges you to take action.
Words are cheap, but actions are life changing. If you really want to help a friend, challenge them to take action. Don't challenge them toward what you want them to do...challenge them to take action on what you hear within their positive intentions.

You have conversations with people every day, and those individuals are bringing up thoughts and possibilities that could powerfully change their life. Perhaps your friend is referring to a change they'd like to make in their marriage or finances or work-life... challenge them to take one step of action that very day.

It could sound like this...

- *"What would it look like to take action on that today?"*
- *"How could you get started on that?"*
- *"Have you thought about setting a goal in that area of life?"*
- *"What does your action plan look like?"*

A true friend is courageous in asking these action-oriented questions as a way to provoke others toward life change. Remember... it's not about what you desire, but about what the person is already expressing as their aspiration.

5. A true friend walks with you...even through the mess.
It's easy and fun to be friends with people who have everything together. When their marriage feels connecting, their kids are doing great in school, and they're excelling in the workplace, friendship is centered upon celebration and enjoyment of life.

Yet, when life goes sideways, the challenge is to continue walking alongside your friend with a desire to 'be with' and resist the desire for a quick fix. There are so many seasons in this life that are painful and life altering. If you haven't experienced any of them yet, it's only a matter of time.

That's not meant to sound doomsday-ish or melodramatic. It's just the truth. At some point or another, we all experience loss, brokenness, and pain in some form or fashion.

Have you experienced…?
- A broken relationship or divorce
- Job loss or bankruptcy
- The death of a loved one (parents, child, etc.)
- Physical illness or injury
- Mental illness
- Addiction
- Natural disaster

Do you feel the weight of all that? You should. It's real life…and all of us experience it at some time or another. Are you willing to walk with others through the mess of life? This will require a degree of grace that can only be found in true friendship.

How to Walk With a Few
Although it may seem obvious how to develop a friendship such as I've described, I don't want to assume anything. If we really know how to do it, why aren't more of us experiencing it? Perhaps, it's not so much an issue of knowledge, but motivation…and courage.

Perhaps, we're afraid of seeking out true friendship, because we're afraid that we'll be rejected or betrayed in some way. It's true. Courage is required…and it comes from a security in knowing who we truly are and what we've been called to in this life.

Rather than skipping ahead of this next section as though it's a remedial class in "How to Make a Friend", would you be willing to look at the experience through fresh eyes? Would you be open to looking at the rhythms of your life and how they may be preventing you from experiencing the friendship that you long for (and need) in the process of a life launch?

1. **Intentionally choose a few people to walk alongside.**
If you're going to develop close relationships that are supportive and nurturing, you can't have that type of connection with everyone. For some of you, that may seem like I'm encouraging you to play favorites with some people. It's not about favorites. It's about the reality that you can't experience a close degree of intimacy with everyone. You don't have that many hours in the day or that amount of relational bandwidth. It's just not possible.

Therefore, you'll want to intentionally choose a few people to walk with. These bonds will probably develop naturally around some sort of common interest or experience. Maybe, they are your co-workers or fellow church members or guys on the softball team. You'll feel the connection, and you'll want to intentionally invest in that relationship in a different way.

I'm not insinuating that you walk up to them and ask them to be best friends or to 'walk alongside you.' You'll freak them out, and you'll feel like an idiot after it's all done with. Resist that urge if it comes up. The intention is within your mind, and it will be expressed in your actions.

2. **Regularly include them in the rhythms of your life.**
This isn't brain surgery, folks! If you're going shopping, invite them along. If you're going to the movies, ask them to join you. If you're going on vacation, see if they'd like to come, too!

We live such disconnected, individualistic lives that we often forget about inviting others to join us in the daily rhythms. Our self-talk goes something like this…"Why would they want to come with me? I'm sure they have stuff going on. They're busy. They'll just say 'no.'"

By calling someone to join you, you're inviting them to connect with you during what may simply be a mundane act of daily life. Yet, in the process, conversations arise that you may never have when you're out with a larger group of friends. You'll have funny, touching, and even adventurous experiences together.

I'll invite friends to join me anywhere I go! Here are a few experiences I've had with close friends just recently...

- Shopping at an outdoor indie arts market.
- Experiencing fireworks together on the 4th of July.
- Buying a new cellphone for my daughter and myself.
- Flying to New York to an international toy fair.
- Traveling to China to purchase fabric for a business.
- Serving people in southern Indian villages.

Some of these experiences were rather ordinary, and others were quite impactful. No matter what...they were more enriching and enjoyable because I was with people I love and care about.

With each experience I have with this small group of friends, my relationship is growing more and more powerful. I'm walking with them, and they're *walking* with me.

3. Courageously allow them into your inner world.
The life-changing moments begin to occur when you're willing to allow them into the sanctuary of your soul. This is the place that very few people have ever been allowed to tread. It's the sacred region of your heart that holds what is most precious.

- Your victories and defeats.
- Your pain, loss, and brokenness.
- Your scars and open wounds.
- Your secret addictions.
- Your hopes, dreams, and aspirations.
- Your longings for a different kind of life.

For many of us, these are the scariest things to share with another human being. We don't want to be laughed at or fixed or discounted. We long for someone to listen and truly hear us...not just our words, but our hearts.

When was the last time you shared any of these things with a friend? When have you created a safe place for others to share these things with you?

Allowing people into your inner world is intentional, and it requires courage. Yet, it's also the only way that powerful relationships are developed.

4. Willingly ask how you can support them.

Oftentimes, people don't know *how* to ask for help. By extending the offer (and really meaning it), you're saying that you truly care about this person. In the midst of your busy life, you are communicating that they are valuable and that you want to invest in them.

There's nothing better than having someone invest in us.

Although it may feel uncomfortable and even humbling, it creates a bond that you'll never forget. I look back over the last few years of my life, and I'm blown away by the support that I've received by a close circle of friends...

- Literally 'walking' miles with me as my life imploded.
- Helping me move twice during a 6-month period of time.
- Encouraging me with their words and presence.
- Referring me to new clients.
- Cheering on our family as we reconciled.

I'll never forget these experiences. Without the support of true friends, I would have never made it through the darkest moments of my life.

This is the time when you need a strong circle of friends the most.

If you're looking to re-launch your life, don't try to do it on your own. Look for people you can walk with...and who will walk with you.

5. Expectantly call when you need help.
The bottom line is...you need people. Everyone needs each other. Life is not meant to be lived alone. It's just not the way we were created, and it doesn't work well. Yes, there are different personalities with differing degrees of extroversion and introversion.

In fact, many people wouldn't realize it, but I'm slightly introverted. After a few hours with a group of people, I need some space. I need to refuel and re-energize...alone or with one other person. Yet, I'm very clear about the fact that I need other people, and other people need me.

I'm learning that when I need help, I need to ask for it. People can't read my mind.

- When I need a hug, I ask my wife to give me one.
- When I need physical help with a project, I ask a friend.
- When I need encouragement, I'll call someone close to me.
- When I need advice, I'll sit down with a confidante who is able to see things from multiple angles.

If I didn't ask for help in these situations, I wouldn't receive it. Although it is a wonderful experience when someone reaches out to me to see if they can help in some way, the reality is that I need to pick up the phone and take the first step.

Life Happens
Walking with others through a life launch (and life itself) is more enriching than anything else in this life. Relationships are beautiful...and they are also challenging and ever-changing.

If a relationship doesn't go through a deepening phase (often characterized by some sort of challenge), it will continue to remain in a rather superficial state of 'niceness.' The question is...will both individuals be committed to working through the relationship in the face of whatever challenge or conflict arises?

As you know, oftentimes the answer is "no."

I'm sure you've experienced relationships that were close and connecting in the past, but you don't speak the person anymore (or as often) because of some sort of issue that arose between you. You were defriended on Facebook, you erased him or her from your cellphone, and you avoid attending events where they may show up.

What happened? Life happened...and one (or both) of you are unwilling (or unable) to deal with it. You weren't able to see your part and apologize and forgive. And/or, they weren't able to do the same.

I want to challenge you to take that step of reconciliation...owning whatever your part is and seeking to clean up the mess. You may not be close friends like you were in the past, but you'll both feel free to move forward. You won't be intertwined with bitterness and resentment.

On the other hand, maybe you will be close again.
It *is* possible.

If it's possible for my wife and I to reconcile and have an amazing marriage after I imploded my life through an affair, I completely believe that you can work through a friendship that isn't what it used to be.

If you want true friends who are willing to walk with you through the mess of life, it requires that you're intentional about investing in them. Are you willing?

The Seven Spheres of Transformation

section 3

As you experience a life launch, there are seven key areas you'll want to address. Although your initial motivation for a re-launch may be found in a particular area of your life (i.e., a job loss, bankruptcy, divorce, etc.), I strongly recommend that you take a holistic approach.

Our lives are not comprised of disconnected parts that never touch, overlap, or impact the others.

If you are recently divorced, don't think that this won't impact the other areas of your life. Take a close look. It's not only impacting your family, but it's reverberating into your finances, friendships, physical health, and your spirituality. The same thing is true if you've walked through a significant painful or depleting experience in any area of your life.

1. You are a holistic being.
You have been created in such a way that your mind, body, and soul is interconnected. When you experience success, all of your being receives the benefit. When you hit a rough patch in life, every part of you is impacted. Don't think that you'll only need to address the area that's in immediate pain.

2. You have a great opportunity when you hit bottom.
When you have a 'rock bottom' experience, you have an incredible opportunity to re-think your approach to life in general. Rather than seeing it as horrific, I want to challenge you to see it as a chance to re-engage life with a fresh perspective and vigor. Don't just sit there...examine all the areas of your life so you can take action!

3. Your life launch depends on "The Process of Intention."
Every single one of these Seven Spheres is essential to your life launch. Although one of them will seem more important in the beginning, you'll eventually want to use the five questions from The Process of Intention to reflect deeply on each sphere. No matter what area of your life you want to experience significant change, the five questions will guide you toward action.

The final section of this resource has been written in a way that you can jump around from chapter to chapter. They don't necessarily build on one another. If you find that you're most interested in processing through your marriage, jump directly to Romance. If you're more concerned about your finances, turn to Money and Possessions. Feel free to use the table of contents in the front of the book to discern what's best for you.

Ultimately, you'll want to read through all Seven Spheres, because re-launching your life truly impacts every facet of your being.

Life Passions
chapter 09

With a clipboard in one hand and a sharp number two pencil in the other, my teacher walked around the room asking us about the future.

"David, what do you want to be when you grow up?"

Most of the class answered with the typical jobs that fascinate kindergartners... policeman, nurse, fireman, or doctor.

Not me.

There was something else that fascinated me. I was interested in adventure, getting my hands dirty, and finding cool stuff that no one else wanted.

"Garbage man!" I said resolutely.

"Garbage man?" she asked. "Are you sure about that?"

"Yep!" I said proudly as the other kids giggled.

Maybe my kindergarten teacher was concerned about the appearance of this on my school records or the embarrassment of my parents or the possibility that it may actually come true.

The term 'sanitation worker' had not yet been devised...nor was the pay for this position as good as it is these days. It wasn't exactly a respected profession...but I didn't care.

As I grew up, I'd come up with a different answer each year, but a few of them really 'stuck' inside me. These were professions that stood out from the myriad of options arising during my school years. As I look back on four particular careers I was excited about at different points in my life, I can see an underlying passion that is still within me today.

- **Garbage man (kindergarten)**
  The truth is I love looking at old stuff. There's something about rummaging through what others would consider trash that enlivens my soul. Whether it's my grandparents' garage, an estate sale, or something that's been dumped on the side of the road, my heart jumps with excitement at the possibility of discovering a treasure. The idea of picking up what others don't want and turning it into something useful or artistic continues to fascinate me.

- **Basketball player (7th grade)**
  Michael Jordan was blowing everyone away with his skills on the basketball court, and I was enamored with the possibilities for my own life. I played basketball constantly, and my family and I had season tickets to Western Kentucky University's basketball teams – both the men's and women's. Although I didn't exactly excel during high school, I enjoyed the competition. Even now, one of my greatest strengths in life is my competitive nature – not a need to be better than everyone else, but a desire to constantly improve and be my best.

- **Photographer (high school)**
  During my freshman year of high school, my grandparents gave me my first SLR camera...a Minolta x-370. I joined the photo team in my journalism class, and I began capturing images for the newspaper and yearbook. When my family and I moved from Ken-

tucky to Lodi, California, when I was 16 years old, we found the high school with the best photojournalism department in the area. I immediately excelled, won several awards, and even worked at the local newspaper. Ultimately, I wanted to be a Sports Illustrated photographer, but I felt a distinct shift in my heart during my senior year. Although I didn't stay on that path, photography helped me pay for college, and I am an avid photographer even today.

- **Pastor (college)**
  I chose to attend a Christian college with my eyes set on being in ministry as a pastor at a church. I wasn't exactly sure what that would look like, but I was passionate about seeing people experience tremendous life change. After graduating from college, I did become a pastor for a number of years, but I eventually experienced tremendous burnout. Despite the fact that I'm no longer a pastor at a church, I am committed to helping others discover a rich, meaningful life.

It's amazing to look back at the careers that I wanted to have (or did have) and see how there is an underlying passion that's still present in my life. It's so clear to me that I'm passionate about...

- Discovering items that are trash in the eyes of others and turning them into something useful or artistic in my own home.

- Being competitive with myself as I seek to grow as an entrepreneur, communicator, and even as a husband and father.

- Capturing photographic images that help others (and myself) to remember special moments and seasons of life.

- Helping others experience a re-launching of their life so that they can have the life they've always wanted.

If you and I have the opportunity to sit down and talk face to face, one of these four passions (among others) will probably come up in our conversation. I would probably mention the seven foot tall, broken windmill that I rescued from my neighbor's trash, painted it bright orange, and placed it in the corner of our living room. I may talk about what I'm learning as a husband and father. Perhaps, I would show you some recent photographs on my iPad and share what they mean to me. Or, maybe I'd ask you about your life and how you're doing…wanting to inspire you to live the life you truly want.

These are some of my passions, and they bring life to my soul.

A Deep and Unending Love

There are passions within you that have been present for a very long time. That's why they're called life passions. These are not passing fads that come along for a few months or even a year and drift away. I'm talking about an affection or affinity that has been present for years… perhaps your entire life.

A life passion is *a deep and unending love for an activity or experience that compels you to bring your very best to this life.*

These passions are interconnected to your identity and who you have been uniquely created to be. It's not the activity that's as important as the deep love that's pouring out from within you when you're involved in it.

It's more about who you are 'being' than what you are 'doing.'
The passionate 'doing' flows out of your 'being.'

This points to a difficult challenge within our culture. Throughout our school years, we are asked, "What do you want to *be* when you grow up?" The person asking the question is looking for an answer in the form of a career or job. They're not looking for us to answer with our identity, which is the 'being' of our existence. They want us to answer with a 'doing' type word.

They are assuming that a particular career can define us…our 'being.'

Listen…"What do you want to *be*?"
We should change the question to either…

- *Who* do you want to be? (passion and character)
- Or, what do you want to *do*? (job and career)

Do you see the difference? We'd serve our children well by helping them unearth their passions rather than thinking about what job they'd like to have. Although this may seem just like semantics, the reality is that we grow up thinking that a career defines us or gives us a certain level of significance. It's our passions that are a true indication of the greatness within us.

Your life passions allow you to bring a level of giftedness to the world at large and specifically to the people around you that no one else can bring. When you're living out your life passions, you are living your life in a distinct way that is creative, powerful, and beautiful. These passions allow you to bring your very best to the table.

There have been periods of time when I'm more focused on a particular passion than another, but that doesn't necessarily mean that the other passions are any less important to me. There is a natural ebb and flow to my interests or attention to a particular activity or experience, but the underlying passion for such things remains rather constant over the long haul.

Although some people are dead set on keeping their life passions and daily 'work' separate, I think that's absolutely ludicrous. Most who hold this perspective indicate that they don't want to ruin their passion by turning it into a job.

Here's my take…I never want another J-O-B again in my life! I want to live out my passions during my best days, and I don't want to wait until I'm 65 years old to do what I really want to do with my life.

For most of us, a job sounds like…

- Something you often put up with from 8am to 5pm (or longer).
- A place where you have to stay in line and play by the rules.
- Work that you perform so that you can get a paycheck.

- Daily toil you endure as you look forward to the weekend.

Although this may be overstating the case a bit, I bet you can relate to what I'm saying. Most people have a job, and very few people are making a passionate living (i.e., finding a way to get paid doing what you really want to do).

Are you courageous enough to discover and live out your passions no matter what it takes? Are you willing to set aside some of your assumptions about work in order to find the life you truly want?

Rediscovering Your Life Passions
I've taken the time to get clear about my life passions…how about you? Can you articulate them in a few sentences? If you know what they are, have you been living them out daily or have you allowed them to become dusty and deteriorated?

If we ignore our passions long enough, they'll go dormant and will need to be jumpstarted through a process of exploration. Let's explore several questions to (re)discover your passions and ignite a fire within you…

- **What activity do you love so much that time seems to fly by?**
  What is it about this experience that is most engaging? Is it really the activity itself or it something that's an integral part of the experience?

  When I was a kid, I loved to re-arrange my bedroom about once a month. Although I do enjoy the décor aspect, I was most interested in mapping out the most strategic way I could organize all my furniture. The experience was more about the strategy and organization than it was about decorating.

- **What is it that gives you so much pleasure that you are oblivious to everything else around you?**
  Do you ever feel like you're 'in the zone'? This is when you're so focused and clear in your thinking that nothing else seems to matter.

For me, it's when I'm speaking in front of an audience on how to live a rich and meaningful life. There's something so extraordinary about preparing a talk and then standing up to deliver it with passion, humor, and challenge. It's as if time stands still every chance I get to speak into the lives of a group of people.

- **What experience do you enjoy that transcends mere personal pleasure and benefits those around you?**
  Most life passions bring benefit to our friends and family in ways that we may not even realize. When we bring our very best to this life, we're bringing something that is beautiful to people around us.

  In my own life, my greatest hope is that I will inspire positive life change in those who come in contact with me. As I model a life of perpetual transformation, share what I'm learning, and encourage others as they courageously live out their passions, I'm not only experiencing great personal pleasure, but I'm benefiting countless others.

- **Why are you here on this earth?**
  Is life just about accumulating as much 'stuff' as possible or being entertained until we die? Or, is it about something with greater depth? My guess is that you know there's something powerful at work here. We haven't been designed for a life of mere self-gratification.

  I believe your life passions are connected to your purpose here on this earth. I believe that God placed those unique passions within you to enjoy and serve people who are in need of what you have.

  Our life passions and our interdependence on one another provide an overwhelming opportunity for connection and relationship. Although there is often a need to monetize our passions to support ourselves, I believe that they've been placed within us so that we can invest them in others. Why are you here?

Making a Passionate Living

After leaving my wife and resigning from my leadership role within the non-profit I founded, I had $3,000 in cash and a credit card with a $32,000 limit. Even though I knew I could last quite awhile with this amount of money, I had to start generating significant income sooner than later...especially since I was going to have to pay spousal and child support relatively quickly.

For the first week or so, I just tried to get my bearings. My new 'love' and I moved into a small apartment, and I was doing my best to manage the emotional roller coaster that came with imploding my life.

As I slowly came to a place where I was gaining some sense of stability, I began contemplating my next steps vocationally. For 10 years, I had been living out my passions in a flexible work environment. For the last five years, I was essentially my own boss as I led the organization on a day-to-day basis. I was accustomed to a great deal of flexibility and autonomy in my ability to make decisions quickly. I mulled over my options...

- **I could start another non-profit.**
  Because I left my wife and the last non-profit under less than desirable circumstances, this option seemed highly unlikely.

- **I could work for a corporation.**
  In southern California, there are thousands of companies in need of sales, marketing, or management candidates each week...but this sounded like utter hell. Right out of college, I worked in a corporate environment at a paper distribution company, and I thought I was going to die. Thankfully, my therapist and close friends thought this option would be suicide.

- **I could leverage my passions to start something new.**
  With financial resources in my hands (cash and credit), I had some time to get something up and running. I started by launching a website offering my coaching or consulting services, and I emailed an announcement to a list of about 400 contacts. I knew

that I'd get tons of hate mail back (for leaving my wife and the nonprofit), but I only needed one person to believe in me. And...I was right. Lots of hate, and one person who contacted me with an opportunity. He and I have become close friends since then, and we've travelled all over the world together in the last three years.

Unfortunately, that first coaching/consulting business didn't go anywhere, but it gave me the contacts to keep moving forward. I jumped from one opportunity to another...staying focused on my life passions...and open to whatever came my way.

Within six months, I started a boutique marketing company (8TRACKstudios) with a friend. Although he moved on with other opportunities, I eventually pulled together an incredible team that includes a graphic designer, web developer, commercial photographer, and videographer. We provide strategic consulting to businesses in regard to their marketing communications and produce anything they need (branding, web development, videos, and more).

This allows me to use one of my skills (creative communication) and affords me the flexibility to write and speak on the subjects of life transformation as well. I'm living out my passions, and I'm being compensated financially in the process.

My decision shouldn't necessarily be your decision. In fact, you probably have different (or more) options in front of you than I did. I was in a unique position, and so are you. The key is that you are aware of your options.

Oftentimes, we don't think we have options, and we give in to whatever is most familiar or convenient to us. We don't allow our minds to think outside of the norm so that we can experience new things.

When I was growing up, my dad worked for the government for almost 20 years, and my mom was an administrative assistant in the banking and loan industries. Both of them were very reliable in their roles, and they provided for our family faithfully.

Key words...reliable and faithful. They weren't entrepreneurs or overly adventurous when it came to careers.

Their stability was comforting as a child, but it also limited my mind in terms of what I thought was possible in this life. I never even thought about starting my own business until I imploded my life and found the other options less than appealing. Fortunately, I had the example of a few entrepreneurial friends to catch a glimpse of what that might be like. I decided that it was the best option for me, and I've supported my family and enjoyed the journey in the process.

That may or may not be the best option for you.

Life Passions: The Process of Intention

As we encounter each of The Seven Spheres of Transformation, I want to invite you to reflect on the questions in The Process of Intention. These questions are designed to help you be intentional about re-launching this area of your life.

1. Who am I?
If you need to, go back to Chapter 4 and remind yourself who you are. You are not your job. You are much more than that. Who are you in regard to your life passions?

2. What do I want?
When it comes to living out your life passions, what do you truly want? If you were rich and didn't need any money, what would you spend the majority of your day doing? If you knew that you couldn't fail, what would you want to do with your life?

Get clear about your life passions and find a way to have someone pay you to live them out. This may involve starting something new, or it may look like changing careers. Get a mental picture of your preferable future...specifically when it comes to how you invest your time each day.

3. What truths will keep me focused?

As soon as you get clear on your vision, lies will come streaming into your mind and heart. Kick them out! They have no place in your life. Find the truth. Amass a briefcase of evidence to fight off those lies. Embrace the truth that you have been created with incredible passions, and you deserve to live them out during the best years of your life.

4. How will I take action?

Without action, all this clarity will go to waste. Pull out a piece of paper, and start making a list of action steps to get you closer to living out your vision. Don't be a wimp and chicken out now. This is where you tap into the Courage that's available to you.

5. Who will walk with me?

The truth is that you can't do it alone. You're going to need someone (or a group of people) to walk with you on the journey of living out your life passions. Who is it? You may need a different person as a resource and support for each of The Seven Spheres of Transformation. Who is it for your life passions? Who do you know who is clear on their passions, and they're living them out daily? Ask that person if you can meet for coffee and talk about what's going on in your life. Ask them to walk with you.

Today is the day. There's no need to waste anymore time working a dead-end job that doesn't allow you to invest your life passions into your daily work. Yes...sometimes we have to do something we don't want to do during a season of life in order to get where we truly want to be. That's okay...but don't use that as an excuse to allow those life passions to be dormant any longer.

Get clear. Get a plan. Get someone to walk with you. There are passions within you that our world is in desperate need of experiencing, and only you can bring them to the table.

Romance
chapter 10

From the time I was 16 years old, I wanted a wife. With each girl I was interested in, I would ask myself the question…"Could she be the one?" There was something about the companionship of a woman (ahem… girl) that was intriguing and attractive to me. I loved the conversation and the connection that was possible, and the playfulness wasn't too bad either.

When my first girlfriend dumped me, I was absolutely devastated…crying and snotting all over the place. And, I was even more crushed when my second 'wife-to-be' in high school called it quits as well.

Thankfully, I headed off the college in southern California where I could start dating like crazy! Nothing was going to stand in the way of me finding the woman of my dreams.

First, there was the 'older woman' (my welcome week counselor) whose father turned out to be one of the college's board members…not a good choice to break up with her. Then, I dated a gal who was in every one of my classes…which was mildly troublesome after we broke up. Next, I went after her good friend…so we had to date in secret. After that, I was hot on the trail of an upper-class redhead who would hardly share anything about herself. Soon after, I was making out with a gal named Betsy that was super-hot, but she didn't want to commit to a relationship.

That would have been a dream for most guys, but I wanted a wife!

In the midst of all my woes, I commiserated with one of Betsy's friends who was way out of my league...her name was Laura. This gal had a curly, golden mane that cascaded down upon her shoulders and framed her gorgeous, bright smile. Our friendship soon turned into 'more' when I asked her out to dinner. Subsequently, we went out every night for 3 weeks straight, and I told her I loved her...and was going to marry her.

As you can imagine, that went over quite well.

Thankfully, she overlooked my craziness and agreed to the possibility of marriage. Within three months of our first date, I was sitting in her parents' living room asking her dad for her hand in marriage. I'm not sure he would have agreed if he would have known about all my ensuing tomfoolery, but he went along with the plan.

The next day, I scraped together all my spare change and headed down to the fanciest mall around to purchase an engagement ring. Less than $2,000 didn't get me more than a speck of a diamond at that snazzy place, but I was proud of it...and I was hoping Laura would be as well.

She said "yes", and we were married 11 months later.
I was 21, and she was 22...practically kids.

Our first year of marriage was wonderful, but in the years to come, we soon found ourselves focused on separate things. We got along great, but our intimacy was waning. With my passion funneled toward the non-profit I founded and her focus on her job as a teacher and our two children, we were practically up for the "Roommates of the Year" award.

15 years into our relationship, I was sick and tired of our marriage, and I wanted a passionate romance. I wanted a different type of relationship, so I set my eyes on my wife's best friend.

The Relationship I Longed For...
There were times when I would fantasize about the possibilities of a different relationship. Although I loved my wife, I longed for something that was different than what I had. I wanted...

- **A friend to experience an adventurous life.**
  My greatest desire was to have a companion who would try things that were new and different. I wanted to be with someone who would walk on the edge of life and shine a smile while doing it.

- **A partner to join me in making a positive impact.**
  I longed for a co-worker to lock arms with me as I changed the world for the benefit of others. The idea of envisioning and planning fresh strategies for a non-profit venture was so invigorating.

- **A lover to be emotionally and physically intimate.**
  My hope was to find someone who I connected with on a deeper level and experience the resulting sexual passion. I wanted to share my hopes, dreams, failures, and frustrations with someone...and be present to hear the same from them.

- **A co-parent to prepare children for our great big world.**
  I wanted to be on the same page with someone in the process of raising children. My hope was that I could be an equal as we invested in their young lives.

Whenever I compared my wife to someone else, she would always come up short. I could see more of these qualities in someone else than I could see in her. I'd watch TV, and I'd see women who embodied adventure. I would talk to a woman at church, and I'd see her passion to make an impact in this world. I would meet someone for the first time, and I'd feel the spark of infatuation that was so fascinating.

As you know, I pulled the trigger, and I left my wife to be with another woman...who left me six weeks later. Within a few days, I checked myself into a psych ward to deal with the reality that I was alone and without a career. After finding my own apartment about 30 minutes away from my family, I soon came to my senses and apologized to my wife and set the trajectory of my heart back toward her.

This process allowed me to unpack some truths about my marriage and romance that I was completely blind to. There was something powerful about hitting the bottom of my life and looking up. It gave me a different viewpoint, and I was challenged to take some action steps that I would never have imagined in my previous life.

The Reality of Romance

Most of us (including me) grow up with a fantastic view of romance and marriage. I use the word 'fantastic' in the truest sense...having to do with fantasy. We watch movies and TV shows about beautiful people who meet in adventurous circumstances, enjoy incredible sex from day one, and then live happily ever after doing interesting things each and every day.

Although I knew this scenario isn't true to life, I still bought into it. It's so hard to resist the illusion that comes with a carefully scripted romance and resulting life of intrigue. Isn't my marriage supposed to be one day of excitement after another? Isn't my wife obligated to find me interesting even when I have bad breath and a cranky attitude? Shouldn't I live from one high to another in my marriage?

All fantasy.

Whether you're wanting to get married, already married, or wish you weren't married, here's the reality of romance that I learned from a rock-bottom vantage point.

- **Get healthy for yourself.**
  No matter if you're single and looking or struggling with your marriage, the first step to having the romance you want is to get healthy for yourself. You're not changing your life for your spouse or your kids. You need to want it for you.

  When I was living alone and I wasn't sure if I was going to get back together with my wife, I had to decide whether or not I was going to pursue emotional, spiritual, relational, and physical health. And, was I going to do it for *me*...or for the possibility of getting back together with my wife?

If it was going to work, it had to be for me. There was no guarantee that she would ever want to take me back. I decided to focus on my own health no matter what.

After working 70-80 hours a week as a workaholic for years, I knew something needed to change. I started going to therapy twice a week, received a brain scan, started taking anti-anxiety meds, and changed my diet and exercise.

For the first time in my adult years, I truly started enjoying life.

After several months of change, I could feel the difference. I was more connected with the few friends that were willing to walk with me. I was losing weight and feeling more energy. I was releasing anger and resentment toward those who had attacked me after leaving the non-profit. I was forgiving the woman who left me, and I was forgiving myself for making such a wreck of my life.

This wasn't for anyone else but me. I needed to get healthy if I was going to have a great life...whether I was living with my wife and kids or not.

How about you? What aspects of your relational life are unhealthy? Where are you holding on to resentment, anger, and a lack of forgiveness? In what ways are you controlling, manipulative, or passive aggressive? Are you willing to seek help to get healthy?

Rarely are we able to move toward health on our own without the assistance of a trained third party.

- **Initiate what you want in the relationship.**
  I was sitting around for over 10 years of our marriage waiting for my wife to be the adventurous, sexy partner I wanted her to be. I would get unbelievably frustrated when she wouldn't meet my expectations, but I never even thought about leading the way with what I wanted.

  As we started to re-connect, I began a little experiment. Instead of me waiting for her to be adventurous, I suggested something that would bring out the adventure in both of us. (Now, my idea of adventure and your idea may not exactly be the same.) Instead of going out to eat at our usual spots, I suggested somewhere different. Rather than shopping for clothes at the some old places, I encouraged us to try a new store with a different style. This continued on and on…from our home décor to outdoor activities to even taking our entire family on a two-week humanitarian trip to India.

  You know what happened?

  My wife joined along in the adventure. Of course, I needed to be sensitive to her level of comfort with some of the things I suggested, but generally she was up for the new experience.

  You know why?

  Because she saw how excited I was about the adventure. As she saw me modeling a new kind of life, she embraced the benefits. My renewed level of excitement was not only beneficial to our relationship, but it was attractive to her. She wanted to join in.

  This was not only true about my desire for adventure, but the same thing played out in the areas of emotional intimacy, sexuality, spirituality, and serving others. It was unrealistic for me to think that she needed to be the one to initiate what I wanted to experience in our relationship.

  When I wanted to feel more intimate, I initiated by sharing my feelings more. When I desired a different sexual experience, I encouraged us to try something new. When I wanted to connect with God together, I suggested how we could do that. And, when I wanted her to join me in serving others, I created space for her involvement.

Are there things that you want in your romantic relationship that you've been waiting around for someone else to bring to the table? Are you waiting for the other person to change so that you'll finally be able to do something you enjoy? If so, are you wiling to initiate and go first? Are you willing to create space for them to join in at their level of comfort?

- **Serve your partner rather than expecting them to serve you.**
The word 'serve' is underutilized outside the context of a restaurant or bar, but it's core meaning is life-giving within a relationship. To serve someone means that you're setting aside your desires in order to meet the needs of another person.

Frankly, I love it when my wife serves me.

I grew up in a rather traditional home where my mom took care of most of the cooking, cleaning, laundry, and home-oriented chores. That is...until she taught me how to do many of those things. Although I had been schooled in how to carry out many of these duties, I quickly fell into a pattern of allowing my new wife to take most of it on.

She cooked while I waited for it to be done. She cleaned, and I pointed out what could be done differently. She did the laundry, and I complained when something wasn't the way I wanted.
I'm making myself out to be quite the ogre which isn't completely true, but I did rely greatly on her willingness to serve me and our family.

A few years before my departure from our home, I heard a seminar presenter suggest, "If there is something to be done in the home, the husband should see it as his responsibility. If there are dishes to be done, he needs to get started. If there is cleaning needed, he needs to pick up a rag. He should be thankful if his wife joins with him."

I wasn't exactly onboard with this notion, and I hoped that my wife wouldn't get wind of it.

Yet, as I was reconciling with my wife, I had a new level of motivation to put his words into action. I started living it out. Instead of acting as if I didn't see the sink full of dishes, I picked up the scrubber and went to work. Rather than relying on her to get the kids ready for bed, I started helping out with anything that needed to be done.

Honestly, she still does way more than I do. She is an incredible servant, and I'm constantly learning from her willingness to sacrifice for the benefit of others. But…I have taken *huge* ground from where I was. I am stretching myself to find new ways to serve and honor her.

The result? A great degree of connection between the two of us. She's incredibly thankful, extra energetic, and more attracted to me as her husband. And, I'm exponentially more grateful for all she does for our family.

- **Be the partner you want him or her to be.**
  Two people living under the same roof raising two kids doesn't necessarily make a family. Yes, we would check the 'married' box on the census, but I'm not sure we could have honestly claimed to be a partnership.

  Partners are two people who choose to join together for the sake of a common cause. It's an aspect of marriage that I longed for, but I didn't quite know how to obtain.

As I was welcomed back into our family's home (six months after abruptly departing), we started using the language of partnership. In an effort to 'try on' the concept, we'd ask ourselves, "Is this what a partner would do in this moment?" In other words, were we both committed to the same cause in that situation? If we were, what would it look like to be *for* each other rather than against? How would I practically behave if I wanted to support my wife as my partner in that circumstance?

By asking that question, I found that I was responding in new ways. Rather than worrying about what I wanted, I began thinking about what would benefit our partnership. I started thinking *team* instead of thinking *me*.

And, in the same way, my wife naturally followed along...thinking and responding in a similar way. I didn't have to ask her to be my partner, she started doing partner-type things in our relationship. She looked out for me. She was concerned about me. She asked how she could help.

For years, I had been waiting around for her to be my partner when all I really needed to do was express my desire for a partnership and begin by being her partner. Of course, that was stretching and hard work and uncomfortable...but the results were amazing.

- **Set aside selfishness and step up as a co-parent.**
The primary reason why I was willing to allow my wife to do most of the parenting in our family is simple. Selfishness. It takes enormous amounts of physical and emotional energy to love, care for, guide, and discipline two growing children.

Our children are extraordinary. They are accomplished in academics, adept with technology, loved by other adults, and gifted with good looks...but they can be a pain in the rear (just like your kids). Although they are like angels in public, come hang out at our home for awhile. Things can go sideways quickly.

For years, I'd bury my head in work (either at the office or on my laptop) and allow my wife to carry the weight of parenting. It was a constant issue between the two of us...until she finally gave up. She let me focus on work, and she handled the kids.

I was happy at first...but all this changed when I moved out of the house, and I only saw my two children three days a week...for a couple of hours at a time. All of the sudden, I found myself wanting to be more involved in their lives than ever. Instead of texting with someone about work, I began talking with my children. Rather than burying my head in the computer, I was burying them in the sand at the beach.

My heart shifted, because I was missing out on what I used to take for granted. I no longer had the opportunity to tuck them into bed or give them a bath or answer questions during those snuggly, quiet moments. I was living somewhere else.

Even though my wife and I were apart, I was doing everything I could to step up and be the dad I never had been. Things changed all the more as we reconciled and I moved back into our family's home.

If you have kids, are you co-parenting or are you leaving up to someone else? What are you missing out on by giving over the responsibility? Ultimately, what are your kids missing out on?

My guess is that I'm not alone in some of my struggles. With over 50% of marriages ending in divorce in the United States, we have serious work to do when it comes to develop long-lasting, intimate partnerships. Once again, these are my learnings...not necessarily yours. Yet, I'm willing to bet there is something powerful you can draw upon if you're willing to reflect on what I've shared from my own life.

Romance: The Process of Intention
As we encounter each of The Seven Spheres of Transformation, I want to invite you to reflect on the questions in The Process of Intention.

These questions are designed to help you be intentional about re-launching this particular area of your life.

1. Who am I?

As you think about a romantic relationship, who are you? Who have you been created to be? As you reflect deeply, I would venture to say that you'll find that you've been designed as a relational being. Having a desire for romance is part of your hard wiring, and you are capable of experiencing something extraordinary.

Review your divine imprint, strengths, wiring, and story from Chapter 4 in order to get a clear picture of who you are.

2. What do I want?

In order to have an intimate relationship, you need to be sure of what you want. Through my disconnected marriage, I started to develop an understanding of my longings. Are you certain about the type of relationship that you want to have with a significant other? Have you taken time to write down the characteristics of the partnership? Do you have a clear mental picture of the preferable future in regards to a romantic relationship?

3. What truths will keep me focused?

If you're not holding onto the truths about you and the possibility of this relationship, the lies will come flooding in and carry you off course on your life launch. Here's the truth. You are a relational being who has a built-in desire for an intimate relationship. You have the capacity to love and be loved. You past relationships do not determine your future. You have access to Wisdom, Grace, and Power to develop a healthy relationship or transform your current one. As you are learning and growing as a partner, you have the opportunity to experience the relationship you've always longed for.

4. How will I take action?

Standing on your true identity...
Based on your clear mental picture of what you want...

Guided by the truths...
Put together an action plan to re-launch your romance.

For my wife and I, this included removing the TV from our bedroom, weekly date night with a committed babysitter, regular counseling to ensure we're on track, daily conversations about our lives, and individual commitments to continue growing as healthy people.

You action steps will be different. The key is that you must be intentional if you're going to experience growth in your relationship. You can't keep making the same decisions with the same mindset and expect different results.

5. Who will walk with me?

You need someone to walk with you (either individually or as a couple) in order to support you on this journey of relational transformation.

My wife and I are walking with our therapist. He asks me tough questions, and he ensures that my wife keeps a strong voice in our relationship.

In addition, we both have close friends who we can be honest with about the condition of our marriage. Because of what we've gone through, this is a top-plate issue that we want to keep in front of us at all times.

How about you? Do you have someone who can walk with you through the unique season of your relationship? Is it a counselor, pastor, close friend? Remember – you can't do this alone.

Romantic relationships can be one of the most delicate parts of re-launching your life. The people we care about the most have the greatest ability to wound us, heal us, and transform us.

Yet, there's nothing more powerful than a partnership that has been developed by two individuals who are committed to getting healthy, serving one another, and living for a common cause.

Community
chapter 11

I don't feel like I've ever been that good at making friends. I remember a time when I was a little kid, and my family and I were walking through K-mart waiting for the 'blue light special' to be announced. As we rounded an aisle, I noticed a classmate from my elementary school, but I didn't even acknowledge him.

"Hi David," he said with the anticipation of some sort of interaction.

Silence.
No response.

"Do you know him?" my Mom asked.

"Uhhhh…yeah."

"Then, say something back!"

I turned my eyes in his direction and mumbled something that at least met my mother's expectations.

As I look back, I wonder if I was overly shy at that age. Perhaps it was early onset of that whole I'm-embarrassed-to-talk-to-friends-in-front-of-my-parents thing. Or, maybe I was just in a bad mood and I felt like being in my own little world.

Whatever it was...I find myself periodically thinking back on that encounter as an indicator of my challenge to develop friendships. Although I long for the connection and camaraderie that comes with close relationships, the work involved can be daunting to many of us. Think about the reality of our lives...

- **High-tech is replacing high-touch.**
  All the accoutrements of a high-tech society surround us. With a high-speed connection to the digital world, we're able to access every type of media designed to play through our media centers. From music to movies to social networking, it's all right at our fingertips.

  We are longing for connection, but it is easier to numb out with disconnecting digital experiences that provide a quick hit to our psyches. In fact, the more high-tech we become...the more high-touch crimes we'll experience.

- **We don't even know our neighbors by name.**
  As our homes have become a haven from the stressful activity that surrounds us, we often barricade ourselves from the world. Gated communities, block walls and head-high fences, alarm systems, closed blinds, and a "No Solicitor" warning at the front door... all subtle (and not so subtle) signs that we're unavailable to those around us.

  Whatever happened to the "Welcome Wagon" that would stop by your house when you moved into the neighborhood? Where did the block parties and neighborhood watch programs go? What happened to watching one another's kids and borrowing a cup of sugar?

  As a matter of fact, what happened to caring enough about the people around us that we took time to know their names?

- **Distrust is rampant in our world.**
    From unwanted spam in our inbox to identity theft by some guy in Europe to divorce with the person we thought we'd spend the rest of our life with, distrust is widespread.

    When people come to our front door, we're not prone to open it. When an unknown number pops up on our phone, we let it go to voicemail. We're leery of people who make promises (especially those in authority), because we've experienced the result of them being broken. There are all these reasons in our head not to trust the people who are coming in and out of our lives.

Combine those three elements (plus a few more depressing ones), and we've got a recipe for a disconnected culture longing for community. It's not that we don't want relationships. In fact, the opposite is true.

We long for connection.

We are dying for authentic, real-life friendships with people who are committed to walking with us through the ups, downs, twists, and turns of life. We want to be known...not just by our name, but by our story. We want people to care about us so much that it would truly matter if we dropped off the face of this earth tomorrow.

Designed for Community
Not only are we created for relationships, but I believe we are also designed to live in community. There's something different about the concept of living in community than just having friends. The idea of having friends seems a bit disjointed...as if I can be friends with five different people and they wouldn't know each other in any way other than through my occasional stories.

When I think of community, I think of the popular sitcom "Friends" and their choice to do life together as we voyeuristically listen in on their lives. I smile as I think of "Seinfeld" and the antics of Jerry, George, Elaine, and Kramer as they experienced 'nothing' together. And, of course, I can't help but be reminded of the place "where everybody knows your name" – "Cheers." I wasn't even old enough to drink, but I wanted to stop by the bar to hang out with Sam, Woody, and the rest of the guys…not because of the beer, but to be part of the connection they had with one another.

The common element in almost every situation comedy like these is the presence of community.

These are not disconnected friendships or random connections. The relationships that are presented in these TV shows are interconnected in a way that is life-giving and nourishing. There are different personalities represented…some that mesh well and others that drive you absolutely nuts.

In a sense, these people are like a 'tribe' that's made a pact to do life together in the face of the craziness of this world. No matter what comes their way, they laugh, cry, scream, and celebrate about it. They are walking through life together.

Here's what I notice about these tribes…

- **Tribes share a common experience, belief, or values system.**
  Although it may not be explicitly stated, there is a commonality that draws the community together in the beginning. It may be a passion for the environment, a love of shopping, a dedication to a sports team, or perhaps a religious belief. Whatever it is…this commonality is the sticky factor that initially allows the group to develop.

  If someone tries to connect in the community without that stickiness (i.e., without having the same experience, belief, or values), most likely the person won't stick around. They'll soon drift away because of a lack of commonality needed to adhere to the other group members. Much of this is invisible to those who are unaware of the dynamics of a community. They just sense that the person was a bit out of place.

- **Tribes have a purpose or mission (stated or unstated).**
Most officially organized groups have a stated purpose or mission statement that is quite clear…civic clubs, churches, and business associations. (Whether or not they live it out is another issue.) Ironically, many of us avoid pledging allegiance to such groups, because we feel as though membership may require something of us.

Despite our intrepidation for organized groups, we are drawn to the clarity that comes from a purpose that is lived out authentically among a group of people with a common vision. The vision may or may not be altruistic in nature. From some, the purpose of their tribe is the experience of adrenaline through some sort of sporting activity. For moms, the mission may be supporting one another through the early years of their children's lives.

For 'un-organized' tribes or communities, this mission is less stated and more understood within the group. It naturally flows out of the common values or experience that the people share.

- **Tribes have a visionary leader (without much of a title).**
One again, this leadership is not generally stated, but it comes to bear through the natural development of the group. Sometimes, the tribe takes shape through the vision of someone who desires to see a group come together for a particular purpose. At other times, the group has naturally assembled and someone steps up to assume a role of leadership.

This isn't necessarily through some sort of self-proclaimed leadership speech. It can be as simple as being the first to share an idea or the person that organizes everyone or the one who is most reliable. Whoever it is and however it comes together…most tightly knit tribes have a leader who emerges to create a greater sense of community.

All of this can sound like a bunch of sociological-mumbo-jumbo, but I want you to be aware of how a community (or a tribe) develops so that you can experience the type of connecting relationships that you truly want in this life.

When I hit rock bottom, I had three friends who were willing to walk with me. In a weird way, the four of us became a tribe overnight, and the mission was to save me and help to re-launch my life.

We didn't call ourselves a tribe…but that's what we were.
We didn't state our purpose…but it was very clear.
We didn't appoint a leader…but everyone knew who it was.

The bond that we shared over the course of a year was like no other I've ever experienced. We're all a few years down the road in a different season of life, and things have shifted and changed. My wife and I reconciled, and my family is better than ever. I'm running a marketing business, and my family and I started a children's home in India. And, we started a spiritual community that gathers in our home once a week as well.

As I think about my own life, I recognize that I'm part of several different tribes…each with their own unique purpose and connectivity. I've made an intentional choice to invest myself in the lives of other people. In the process, we all support one another on this journey called life.

Creating Your Own Community
If you're lacking in the area of friendships and community, it's so easy to lay blame on anyone or anything else other than yourself. The truth is that there is something holding you back from making the connections that you long for.

Is it a fear of being rejected?
Could it be a feeling of superiority?
Maybe it's an anxiety over being authentically known by others?
Or, are you more comfortable being alone so everything will go your way?

Getting connected in a healthy, life-giving community is one of the most powerful steps of a life launch. You may find yourself drawing upon the expertise of certain people as you re-launch each of The Seven Spheres of Transformation, but you'll need a tribe who is also genuinely interested in your success.

This doesn't usually come to fruition by happenstance. It requires *intention* on your part to develop what you want. Here's how to get it...

1. Choose to invest in certain relationships.
Instead of randomly connecting with people from day to day and week to week, begin to put effort toward building relationships with a small group of people. These people may or may not be an existing community, and that doesn't matter. You are simply deciding to leverage the limited amount of relational bandwidth that you have on these individuals. You can't develop a close, authentic relationship with *everyone* in your life. It's a matter of choosing people to walk with.

Remember, not everyone you initially invest in will turn out to be part of your ongoing community. People come in and out of our lives at different seasons for a variety of reasons, but you have an opportunity to be a faithful friend.

2. Plan and coordinate intentional gatherings.
The only way that a community or tribe can be developed is if people spend time together. It's within the context of these gatherings that people discover the commonalities among themselves. They begin to make natural connections that can only come through a prolonged experience together. From a BBQ to a day at the beach, any gathering will work. It doesn't have to be fancy or extravagant. The goal is for people to connect with people.

And, if you're the one making the plans, people will be drawn to your genuine initiation. They'll see your effort, and they'll want to be part of what you're up to. This doesn't mean that you're necessarily *the* leader or have to take on some role.

You are simply choosing to go *first*.

Going first is oftentimes the most powerful thing in the process of developing a community. People want to be part of something bigger than themselves, but they're afraid to take that first step. They're afraid of rejection...whether they'll admit or not.

3. Introduce people from different walks of life.
When you've got people together, introduce them! There's nothing I hate more than showing up at a gathering, event, or party, and no one introduces people to one another. I don't know if they think we magically know each other or that we'll be brave enough to extend a hand, but I find more times than not that I'm the one to get people to start connecting.

Think about how you'd like to be treated when you show up at an event where you don't know anyone. My guess is that you enjoy being warmly welcomed, given a cold drink, and introduced to someone. If you are wanting to develop community in your life, the greatest gift you can give someone else is the gift of commonality. Think about what people have in common with one another and introduce them. You'll be creating a level of connectedness that is sure to stick!

4. Be willing to take relational risks.
The greatest roadblock to develop the community of friends that you long for is fear...fear of the unknown, fear of rejection, and fear of authenticity. Yet, if you want *real* relationships that go beyond a surface level, you'll need to take some relational risks.

If your launch pad is strong, you'll be confident in who you are. Remember, your identity is the foundation of your life launch... and your life as a whole. If you are secure in the fact that God has created you with an amazing divine imprint and that you have remarkable strengths, you will be poised for authentic relationships.

When you are honest about your opinions while allowing others to have their own, you won't be concerned about rejection. You'll be secure in your identity.

When you express your care or admiration for someone else, you won't be dependant upon their reciprocal response. You'll be secure in your identity.

When you disclose something challenging about your past, you won't be worried about any potential judgment. You'll be secure in your identity.

If you're looking to develop friendships with people where there's no chance of getting hurt, you'll never find a community. The bottom line is that people will let you down. People will fail miserably, blow it big time, and frustrate you completely…intentionally and unintentionally. You have the opportunity to be secure in your identity and extend forgiveness as you work toward healthy relationships.

The beauty of experiencing compassionate, encouraging community relationships is worth all the effort in the world. With a measure of grace and forgiveness combined with courage, a tribe can be one of the most transformative parts of your life. You have the opportunity to be part of something so much bigger than yourself. You can serve, love, embrace, challenge, extend mercy, and so much more.

Taking It Deeper
The challenge for most friends who hang out on a regular basis (whether they're centered around a sport, political ideology, or religion) is to take things to a deeper level so that they can experience actual 'community'…and not just surface relationships.

"How are you?"
"Fine."

"How about you?"
"Great."

Sound familiar? This type of polite banter is nothing more than a meaningless form of greeting one another in our culture. Unfortunately, much of our conversation doesn't go beyond this. Weather, sports, kids' activities...that's about it.

If you truly want to take your relationships to a deep level to experience authentic community, here's a great start...

- **Listen more and talk less.**
  When you quit talking and start to actively listen, you'll learn a great deal about the other person's hopes, dreams, failures, and frustrations. You're offering them space to process what's going on in life, and you have the potential to help them unlock the beauty that's hidden within them.

- **Celebrate with those who celebrate.**
  When someone experiences something great in their life, are you able to celebrate with them? If you're secure in your identity, you won't feel threatened by their success, and you'll be able to enter into the joy with them. Share their joy, and your joy will come soon enough.

- **Cry with those who cry.**
  Sympathy for those who are hurting is nice (and even expected), but empathy (the ability to share in their pain) is a gift of healing. When you're able to be physically and emotionally present during someone's darkest moments, you will bond in a way that is unique and powerful. There's nothing like walking through a valley with a friend who isn't scared away by our pain.

- **Share deeply from your own life.**
  The quickest way to deepen a relationship is to be appropriately vulnerable with your own life. If you have a dream or ambition, are you willing to share it? If you're fearful about the future, have you courageously asked for support? If you're frustrated or stuck in life, have you been honest with those around you? As you authentically share what's going on inside you, there will be an op-

portunity for your relationships to deepen and your community to bond in life-changing ways.

The reason why most 'groups' never turn into 'community' is simply because it can be scary to be real about what's going on in our lives. In a lot of ways, it's just easier to live a disconnected life...or a semi-connected life where I experience the guise of relationship. We know each other's names and share some of the same experiences, but we don't really know each other.

My guess is...*you want something more.*

As you seek to re-launch your life, it would be wise to be intentional about the development of your friendships and how those can positively impact you. Don't just assume that things will come together in due time. It requires intentionality on your part to develop the supportive, authentic relationships that you need in order to live the life you truly desire.

Community: The Process of Intention

As we encounter each of The Seven Spheres of Transformation, I want to invite you to reflect on the questions in The Process of Intention. These questions are designed to help you be intentional about re-launching this particular area of your life.

1. Who am I?
As you think about developing authentic friendships, who are you? Have you firmly taken hold of the fact that you were created for relationships? Are you clear about the fact that you can't find security or safety in anyone else other than you and God?

2. What do I want?
What types of relationships do you want? Is there a particular set of beliefs, values, or experiences that you want your community to embrace? Are these the type of people you're currently connected with? Why or why not? Maybe you need to carve out an hour from your day to write down your vision of the community

you long to be part of. That tribe may not exist yet, and you might be the person to initiate the connections.

3. What truths will keep me focused?
In the same way that a romantic relationship can be difficult to form if you believe the lies, so can a community of friendships. When you're thinking that people don't like you or you don't measure up or that people are out to get you, it will be virtually impossible to get close to others. The truth is that you are a remarkable individual and God has created other remarkable people to walk in relationship with you. You have the capacity to have supportive friendships, and you're learning every step of the way. Do you believe it?

4. How will I take action?
It is quite clear what it takes to be part of a community. What are your next steps, and are you willing to take them? Do you need to step back from some of the unhealthy people you've been investing in? Are there other people you need to courageously reach out to in order to spend time with? What would it look like for you to go first and initiate a gathering of people? What's stopping you?

5. Who will walk with me?
It may sound a bit odd, but you need someone to walk with you in the process of developing friendships. This is a person who is confident in their identity, and they have no problem developing healthy friendships. That doesn't mean that they have to be the most outgoing person in the world, but you see evidence of a community of relationships in their life. Tell them that you're looking to take some fresh steps in the area of friendships, and ask for their help and encouragement. You'll be glad you did.

Don't buy into the lie that *authentic* relationships are too much work... or even impossible to develop. There are other people in the world that are feeling the same way you are...other couples, singles, single parents, divorcees...who want what you want. Don't give up.

In my own life, 'Community' was the final Sphere of Transformation in which I started to experience significant growth as I re-launched my life. While the reconciliation with my wife happened early on, I found that a restoration of my friendships took much longer. There was a serious lack of trust among people I already knew, and I was hesitant to jump right out there to develop new relationships.

Yet, as I faithfully embraced my true identity as the foundation of my life, I was courageous in making amends and connecting with new people. My wife and I worked as a team to invite people over to our home, and we shared the ways that our life was being transformed. Our authenticity allowed others to open up about their own struggles, and a connection was developed which would have been impossible without our own transparency in the first place.

We're now enjoying some of the most rewarding relationships we've ever experienced, and our sense of community is rich and meaningful.

This *is* possible, and it's available to you.

Money and Possessions
chapter 12

After telling Laura I was done with our marriage and then enjoying a three-day frolic in San Diego with her best friend, I returned home to find the locks changed and all my clothes stuffed into black trash bags and tossed on the driveway. When your heartbroken wife hands you half of the savings and a credit card on the way out the door, your mind starts to think about 'stuff' in a brand new way.

In retrospect, she was incredibly generous to hand over some cash and a piece of plastic that didn't have a penny of debt.

As I drove away in my Ford Focus (which was paid off), my mind started racing to determine my next steps. I held the check tightly in my hands as I realized that this was a precious resource that was going to need to last me for quite some time.

My new love interest and I ended up checking into the "Peacock Motel" about a mile away, and we spent the next day tracking down two very important things...a divorce attorney and an apartment...both of which would need to take credit card. There was no way I was going to part with any portion of that $3,000 cash if I didn't have to.

My strategy was to put everything on credit card and trust that I could pay it off later…either through a lucrative new job or through the sale of our family home.

Over the course of six months, I racked up $33,000 in debt by paying for a divorce attorney, incredible dinners with the new love of my life, our apartment deposit, furniture for our new place, a $6,000 diamond ring, the broken lease penalty after my new love left me, another apartment deposit, and another broken lease penalty when I finally moved back into my family's home. Those were all the big expenses that didn't include daily living expenses such as food, clothes, utilities, therapy sessions at $150 a week, and health insurance at $400 a month.

Debt started to pile up quickly since I didn't have a job, and I was just trying to survive.

Until that point in my life, I had no debt except for one car payment (my wife's van) and our mortgage. My wife and I had been very careful not to purchase things on credit unless we planned to pay them off by the end of the month.

When I chose to implode my life, things changed. I was simply trying to survive…in every area of my life. It's no surprise that money and possessions would need to be a significant part of re-launching my life after making such a mess.

As my wife and I were reconciling through counseling, she made it clear that she wasn't interested in me coming home until that credit card was paid off. I started to think…"I may never move back home if that's the case!" As I developed business opportunities that were beginning to generate income, I started making payments based on an interest-free plan I set up with the credit card company.

Although it's not paid off completely, I'm well on my way. (And, thankfully, my wife welcomed me home before the balance hit zero.)

I'm not sure where you find yourself in terms of income and debt, but I will tell you that there's hope. Amazing things can happen in this area of your life if you're willing to examine how you view your 'stuff' and take intentional action toward getting the life you truly want.

Debt Strangles Your Life

When my wife and I were first married, we had an old hand-me-down couch from my parents that was in less-than-stellar shape. As we were moving to a bigger apartment, we felt like it was the right time to purchase a new living room set. Although we didn't have the cash on hand, a lovely furniture store offered us a no-money-down promotion.

Sound familiar?

We were elated. We could get the furniture we needed and pay it off over the course of the next year without paying a dime of interest.

The green and white striped furniture was delivered, and we couldn't wait to snuggle up to watch a movie together. The pleasure of sitting on our first furniture purchase was unbelievable...that is, until I started to think about the fact that it wasn't really ours.

In reality, it still belonged to the furniture store...until we paid it off.

Every day I came home from work, I couldn't find it within myself to sit on the couch or the chair. Instead, I sat on the floor and leaned up against it. There was something about sitting on that couch that was strangling the life out of me. I couldn't get it out of my head.

It was the fact that we still owed money on it. We were in debt to someone for a measly couch! Within a couple of months we paid off what was due, but I never looked at that couch with affection. It was a powerful symbol of debt in my life.

I'm not sure why I didn't feel that strongly about our car payment at the time, but my aversion to debt on smaller purchases was quite clear. Unfortunately, my dance with debt began once again when I left my wife many years later. I knew things would be tough, but I didn't anticipate how fast it would all pile up.

I quickly found myself experiencing both of the reasons why people in our culture tend to accrue debt.

1. We rely on credit when life goes sideways.
Although my situation may be unique (i.e., racking up $33,000 in debt in 6 months), more and more people are finding themselves with a tremendous amount of debt by relying on credit as a fallback when they lose their job or have an unanticipated expense. If you don't have 3-6 months of reserves set aside, the only alternative in the case of a job loss is credit. Oftentimes, an unemployment check won't cover day-to-day expenses.

I have also found that once someone piles up $5-10,000 in debt during a job loss or prolonged illness, they are more prone to keep adding to the debt after they re-gain employment. It's almost as if the resistance has been removed, and it's easier to just throw it on the card than have restraint.

2. We rely on credit to get things we want…but can't afford.
Almost everyone has made this mistake. You see the clothing, electronic gadget, or couch, and you just have to have it. Everyone around you has this item, and you think you need it, too. Unfortunately, you don't have the money in your bank account to make it happen. It would require saving or getting an extra job or some other creative plan.

You buy it anyway…and you start amassing debt. Sooner or later, you come to your senses, and you realize that you've got to pay for that 'stuff' you don't even use (or own) anymore.

Although there are many issues to address in the process of re-launching this sphere of your life, I want to make sure you're absolutely clear about the way debt strangles the life out of you. As I learned from that simple no-money-down purchase, debt is a vicious beast that lies to you about all the stuff in this world.

It has one intention…to take away your freedom and prevent you from experiencing the joy, peace, and fulfillment that you truly long for in this life.

The Lies I Believe About Stuff
There are lies that pierce our hearts in every one of The Seven Spheres of Transformation, but they are particularly powerful when it comes to money and possessions. We are a consumer culture that relies upon each person's internal desire to make money…and buy things that we don't really need. There are wonderful products that allow us to live a healthy life, but most things marketed to us are simply unnecessary.

There are three lies I tend to believe over and over again…

- **More stuff will make me feel better.**
  When I'm feeling down, depressed, overwhelmed, or anxious, I love to shop. There's something about buying a new outfit that breathes life into my deflated heart…until I get it home. Maybe I'll wear it once, wash it, and add it to the collection in my closet before I realize the fleeting 'high' quickly went away.

- **I don't have enough…I need more stuff.**
  There are times when I'm standing at a display counter…oohing and aahing over the latest and greatest technological gadget. I'll spend 20-30 minutes pacing back and forth as I talk myself into the fact that I need this item. I'll come up with a long list of reasons how it will make me more productive and generate income and be the breakthrough I need in that area of my life. All lies.

- **My value is determined by what I own.**
  Living in southern California (or simply turning on the TV for that matter) makes it easy to compare my stuff with someone else's stuff. Although I live in a wonderful 3 bedroom home, I can drive through another city and somehow feel 'less than' because my neighborhood isn't as nice. It's not just limited to my home…it's the newness of my car, the brand of my clothes, the size of my TV, the model of my cellphone, and even the purse that my wife carries on her shoulder.

My guess is that I'm not the only one who tends to buy into these lies. Yes, we need to generate income, and we will continue to purchase products in this life. That's not a bad thing at all. Yet, we have the incredible opportunity to re-orient our thinking around the truth. As you know, the result of believing the lies is a soulless life that lacks true peace.

The truth is that your ability to generate income is a gift from God. God gave you a great personality, wonderful strengths, and the physical and mental ability to work. The truth is that money is not evil. It is simply a tool to purchase physical items and experiences you need. It is a gift to be enjoyed and generously shared with others.

When we start to believe the truth about our money and possessions, we'll gain a freedom to live the life we truly long for…a rich, meaningful life.

The Freedom of Choice
I love freedom. I love the fact that we live a life where we can do whatever we want. Of course, there are repercussions to each of our decisions…some of which end up restricting our freedom and some that produce even more liberty…especially in the area of finances.

For instance, I exercised my freedom when I left my wife, and the freedom was incredible. I was with another woman, and I could spend my time and money any way I wanted to. Because I made use of my freedom in a way that lacked responsibility, I experienced hellish fallout in the process. I ended up all alone…in a psych ward…and a few months later, in a huge amount of dead.

You have the freedom to manage your money and possessions any way that you wish. Feel the freedom, baby! It is awesome.

At the same time, realize the that your decisions will end up producing more freedom…or hardly any freedom at all.

You have the freedom of choice when you…

- Live below your means – choosing to spend only what you earn.
- Don't owe anyone else money – saving up for purchases instead.
- Save/invest for the future – planning for the unexpected.

The future stress that comes with purchasing things that you can't pay for immediately just isn't worth it. The anxiety of not having reserves in place can be taxing to the soul. The interest that comes with debt means you end up paying more than the item is even worth.

Although it can feel so liberating to live a carefree life when it comes to money and possessions, the results end up taking away your freedom. If you want to re-gain the freedom that was intended for your life, you must be intentional.

Choosing to Make Stuff Work for You

As with anything else in your life launch, you're going to need to take some steps that will be uncomfortable and even seem ludicrous in the beginning. One of the reasons why I've addressed debt at such length is because of the pervasive nature of the problem and because most people who are re-launching their lives have significant challenges in the area of money.

If you're ready to get serious, here's a simple path of baby steps that will result in serious life change.

1. Recognize the Source of your resources.

There's something powerful about acknowledging the source of your resources. I'm operating off an assumption that God created you and me with incredible abilities…one of which is the potential to create, build, develop, and administrate.

When I see my life as a gift from God, my attitude immediately shifts from lacking something to being thankful for God's goodness in my life. This causes me to look back upon my identity and see that I truly am a remarkable person…uniquely created by God.

You are remarkable!

Why? Because you have gifts, talents, and a personality like no other person on the planet. Your one-of-a-kind wiring and unique story empower you to do great things in this life that no one else can do.

2. Acknowledge the power of money and possessions.
Let's not underestimate the potential of money to help us or hurt us in this life. In and of itself, it is a neutral resource...yet it has incredible potential.

If we ignore the possibility of being shackled to our stuff, we may find ourselves burdened by a mortgage we can't pay, a boat we don't use, and a credit card payment we can't make.

If we don't pay heed to the opportunity of money, we'll miss out on moments in life when we could leverage our resources for the benefit of others.

Admit that money is a powerful force in your life.
Make an intentional choice as to how you'll use it.

3. Cultivate thankfulness for what you have.
Thankfulness literally means to be full of thanks. This is an ongoing posture of extending appreciation to God for what has been given to you. I've never been a big fan of generalized thankfulness as if I'm just spewing it in every direction. For some reason, I find my degree of thanks increases when I point it toward the One who has given me life to begin with.

Each time you start to compare what you have to someone else, just whisper to yourself, "I am thankful." Although you may find it helpful to recognize that you have been given so much in comparison to so many in the developing world, I find that it still locks me into the comparison game. I want to get out of comparing altogether. I want to be in a place of contentment where I am appreciative for what I already have.

Our family was invited to a WNBA game featuring the Los Angeles Sparks at the Staples Center on the night after the Lakers beat the Celtics for the 2010 NBA Championship. There was still a buzz in the air, and it was amazing to be there...especially since we were sitting on the court. Yes, we were literally sitting on the front row of the entire arena as we watched the game. On top of that, I was sitting next to a Celtics player whose wife happened to star for the Sparks. As bits of confetti were still falling from the rafters, I was in awe of my vantage point.

As I watched the game, my eyes were drawn to the very top row of seats on the opposite side of the court...way up at the very top. A few weeks prior, my son and I were sitting in those seats as we watched an Los Angeles Kings ice hockey match...and we had a great time.

No matter if I'm sitting at the top of the arena or literally on the floor, I can be thankful. Frankly, I'd rather sit on the floor, but I can be content in either place. It's simply a matter of cultivating thankfulness and recognizing that it's a choice that I can intentionally make.

If I choose to love money, I'll never have enough.
If I choose to be thankful for what I have,
I'll find contentment and peace.

4. Become a wise manager of your stuff.
Here's where the rubber meets the road. Are you going to intentionally start managing your resources in a way that will set you up to gain more freedom? Are you going to float through life 'just making it' or are you going to get serious about how to leverage your resources for the sake of good in this world?

Frankly, you probably need some help. Most of us do. You may need to hire a money manager or ask a friend who is already managing their money well or buy a book or go to a seminar. I don't know what will work for you, but you must get intentional if you want to re-launch your life.

Getting the rest of your life on the launch pad and leaving your money and possessions behind is a big mistake. You'll lose the freedom you need to explore this grand life that's out in front of you.

5. Enjoy the fruits of your labor.
There is a great difference between owning your stuff and allowing your stuff to own you. When you take control of your money and possessions, you'll have the power (and freedom) to enjoy the fruits of your labor.

There's nothing like buying something you've saved up for.
There's nothing like delighting in an object you can truly afford.
There's nothing like driving a car that's paid off.
There's nothing like writing a $500 check to a friend who just lost their job.

The enjoyment that comes from living within your means in remarkable. Have you tried it? That's what it means to truly enjoy your stuff.

6. Be generous to those in need.
The most powerful antidote to consumerism and greed is generosity. By opening up your tightly closed wallet and investing in the lives of others, you'll experience the greatest degree of freedom in your life.

If you feel like your possessions own you, give some away.
If you are struggling with making money, give some away.
If you think that there isn't enough to go around, give some away.

Something happens inside of every human being when we willingly give something to another person. It changes our hearts.

An ancient saying goes like this..."For where your treasure is, there will your heart be also." In other words, whatever you choose to invest your money in is what will matter most in your life.

Although I love to enjoy the stuff that's in my life, I derive such great pleasure by being generous. From starting a children's home in India to helping a new friend who is without a home to assisting a family at our church who is struggling and even paying for a friend to fly to their sister's wedding…these are all ways that I've had the privilege of giving to others recently.

My wife and I have intentionally developed generosity in our lives…when we had very little and when we've had more than we needed. The results have been tremendous. We're able to participate in seeing transformation take place in the lives of other people…and we always seem to have enough ourselves.

These steps are the difference between you working for your 'stuff' and the 'stuff' working for you. In the process of re-launching your life, money and possessions will give you more or less freedom to blast into uncharted territories. You don't want to be loaded down on the launch pad with unneeded possessions or heaping debt. You have the ability to get the freedom you need. It will require an intentional process.

Money & Possessions: The Process of Intention
As we encounter each of The Seven Spheres of Transformation, I want to invite you to reflect on the questions in The Process of Intention. These questions are designed to help you be intentional about re-launching this area of your life.

1. Who am I?
As you think about your money and possessions, who are you? Are you a merely a selfish consumer or are you a generous producer?

Don't just focus on your current behavior. Look deep within to discover the true identity that was created within you before you were even born.

2. What do I want?
What type of lifestyle do you long for? Get a mental picture of what that lifestyle looks like. As you close your eyes and see a vision of your preferable future, be less concerned about what house you're living in or what car you're driving.

Focus in on the level of joy, peace, and freedom you long to have when it comes to money and possessions.

Can you feel it? Can you see it? That's what you'll want to move toward.

3. What truths will keep me focused?
It's so easy to buy into the lies that stuff will make us happy and satisfy us deep down inside. We try it over and over again, and it never works. What are the truths about yourself and your stuff that you want to hold on to during your life launch?

Remember that your ability to generate income is a gift from God. God gave you a great personality, wonderful strengths, and the physical and mental ability to work.

The truth is that money is not evil. It is simply a tool to purchase physical items and experiences you need. It is a gift to be enjoyed and generously shared with others.

4. How will I take action?
You have the opportunity to take intentional action. You know that already, but I'm just cheering you on. Depending on your circumstances, you may need to get more information, be inspired, set up a system, develop accountability, or all of the above. Set your goal, and develop a plan to get there.

5. Who will walk with me?
Finally, you will need someone to walk with you. This may be a close friend, your spouse, a financial advisor, or someone else that's experienced in this area of life.

Don't be embarrassed or ashamed. Asking for help is a courageous step toward the life that you truly want.

Creativity and Play
chapter 13

A number of years ago, I seemed to be surrounded by artists. One person after another (gifted in manipulating raw materials into something beautiful) was coming into my life.

Although I had been a photographer for many years, most of my experience was in the area of documenting events through photojournalism. I never really saw myself as a creative person, nor did I find much artistic inclination within my bones.

I do remember taking several art classes and enjoying it...charcoal drawings, some watercolors, high school ceramics, and the ubiquitous doodling during school to relieve my brain from the boredom of subjects I had little interest in.

Since my last high school arts class, I hadn't spent any measurable time focused on creating something for shear pleasure or personal expression. My focus was more on academics, the corporate world, and then starting non-profits to 'change the world.'

"Who has time to sit around and paint?" I'd ask myself. "And, what would I paint even if I did?"

Although few of these newfound friends were professionals, most were creating passionate works of art on the weekends and evenings for the deep sense of pleasure they received in the process. One of my friends named Mark worked for a company selling websites and IT services. In his spare time, he would paint on any surface he could get his hands on…including asphalt. He was becoming well known in our area as an accomplished chalk painter as he re-created masterful works of art at numerous fairs and festivals.

His passion for his art was so contagious that I found myself inspired to create something myself. The only problem was…I didn't have any supplies, and I didn't know where to start.

"Um…hey Mark…I'm thinking about maybe painting something." I couldn't have sounded more unsure of myself. "And…I'm mortified to even walk into an art store to ask what I need to purchase."

The only time I had been more hesitant in my life was the moment before getting my first tattoo. Seriously. Who gets nervous about walking into an art store to buy paint? Well, probably someone who buys into the belief that art is for born artists or those who don't have anything productive to do or people who are 70 and retired.

I didn't seem to fit into any of those categories.

Somehow, I had relegated artwork to the days of my youth, and those days were never to return again. Yet, I found myself being inspired by the wide-eyed wonder of Mark and the others who were serendipitously appearing in my life.

- Jill was creating postcards with her beautiful photography.
- Branin was teaching people how to create pinhole cameras.
- Luke was using graphic design to inspire his clients.
- Lee was building sets with precision and beauty.
- And, Mark was painting anything and everything.

What was I doing? I was trying hard to be successful at the non-profit

I was working for. I was overwhelmed and tired and needing to be re-energized.

"David, it's not that complicated," Mark reassured me. "Head over to the art store and pick up…" He went on to explain the brushes, acrylic paints, and a couple of canvases I would need. In fact, he offered to even go with me!

As I returned home with my bags filled with art supplies, I wanted to get right to work. Thankfully, my family was gone for the afternoon, and I had the house all to myself. Since I hadn't invested in an easel quite yet, I pulled out an old beach towel and laid in on the carpeted floor. I unwrapped the canvas and started placing all my materials around the makeshift workspace.

For days, I had been thinking about what to paint. A landscape? A portrait? An abstract? None of those things appealed to me. For some reason, I kept having robots pop into my head. There was something about a simple, red robot in random settings that intrigued me. All the while, I heard the sucking sound of lies trying to rid me of creative fuel.

- *"Why are you doing this? This is a waste of time."*
- *"You could be spending time doing something productive."*
- *"No one is going to like whatever you create."*
- *"People are going to laugh at you."*

I finally pushed back all the dark voices long enough to unscrew the tubes of paint and get some color on the canvas. From the first stroke of my new brush, I felt an unleashing of something within me. It was a freedom to create anything I wanted. No one was restricting me or telling me what to do. The only boundaries were the edges of the canvas and the creativity within my mind.

Within a couple of hours, I was really enjoying the process, but I heard footsteps approaching our front door. It was my family!

I had to make a split-second decision. Wrap everything up and hide it…

or come clean with the fact that I was trying something new? You see, they didn't even know that I had purchased supplies...nor that I was interested in painting.

"Wow, what are you up to?" My wife asked.

"That's a cool robot, Daddy!" Waverly chimed in.

"Well, I just thought I'd try something new...and painting sounded kinda fun."

They didn't laugh at me or mock me...and it really wouldn't have mattered if they did. This was something I wanted to do for myself. In the following year, I painted small canvases and huge canvases...each with the same red robot in an odd environment. From standing on top of a skyscraper to being surrounded by bright, yellow cats, my red robot was allowing my mind to experience a freedom that was both refreshing and rejuvenating.

What Happened to my Creativity and Playfulness?
Nowadays I sit back and watch my two children play, and they exude a level of creativity that I long to re-capture in my own life...even years after that first painting experience. They have the ability to envision things that don't exist and create worlds to play within for hours. Emerson will build a spaceship with his Legos and protect our planet from the attack of invading monsters...his stuffed animals. Waverly will set up entire bedrooms (within her bedroom) for her American Girl dolls... undressing and redressing them over and over again.

I remember the days when I displayed that level of creativity.

In fact, I recently saw an old home movie from when I lived in Kentucky. My room was decorated with sports memorabilia, artwork, posters, and a hand-made miniature skate park for all my finger-sized skateboards. After seeing that video, I remembered spending hours creating the skate park and imagining myself as Tony Hawk flying over and through each apparatus.

What happened to my ability to envision (and even create) new worlds to enjoy? It's as if the creativity within me had rusted away over the years of neglect. I'm wondering if most adults have that same experience. I'm wondering if we've ignored this amazing resource within ourselves in the name of adulthood and ultimately productivity.

I'm realizing that I've believed a few lies about creativity and play...

1. Performance is more valuable than creativity.
Our world is built on performance. As children move up from year to year, test scores and grades become increasingly important. By the time a young person is entering high school, the need to succeed has been drilled into their brains on so many occasions that there is little time left for mere creativity.

Ironically, it's this creativity that allows us to solve problems in new ways, develop engaging relationships, and nourish our souls. Creative energy results in beauty, inspiration, and wonder...all things that are difficult to quantify or convert into a tangible return on investment. Yet, these intangibles are life-giving in and of themselves.

2. If it doesn't produce a return, it's not worth doing.
Return on investment is in the forefront of many of our minds as we seek to utilize the precious commodity of time and money.

"After an 8-10 hour work day and the kids' homework and the dinner dishes, why would I want to waste my time creating something? I'd rather just plop down in front of the TV and veg out. On top of that, who has the extra money to be spending on art supplies and stuff like that?"

Can you hear yourself?

There's something about needing a clear and definable outcome that makes an experience worthwhile in our culture. Who says you need to create something that's worthy of being sold? Or, why is there a need for it to be 'good enough' to hang in a gallery? And, why would you care about the opinions of others once it's completed?

What about the sheer enjoyment of allowing what's inside of you to flow onto the canvas or through the lens of a camera? Perhaps our need to see a clear return on our investment of time and money is unreasonable. Maybe the return will be found within the rejuvenation of our hearts.

3. Adults don't 'play'...unless it's organized sports.

The brother of creativity is playfulness, and somehow it disappears as we become 'grown-ups.' Our need to succeed in this world requires us to rid ourselves of skipping on the playground, running through the house, and dressing up like a superhero. Those things are just for kids...or are they?

What if we revisited the playfulness of our youth? Would the laughter and freedom and imagination open up our minds and hearts to a new kind of life? Is it possible that the enjoyment of the moment would re-create a fresh perspective?

For many of us, the risk of looking ridiculous in the eyes of others is just too great. We'd rather remain stuffy and boring adults who play softball at the company picnic once a year. We've bought into the lie that says 'play' is for children and a waste of time once you grow up into the real world.

In the process of re-launching your life, creativity and playfulness can unlock parts of you that haven't seen the light of day in years and produce a new degree of enjoyment. One of the greatest deficiencies in the lives of many who are in need of a life launch is a deep lack of joy.

As I lived alone in my apartment for six months without my family, I took stock of every aspect of my life. It became extremely clear that I hadn't enjoyed my life since the early days of college.

During one late-night phone call with my wife, I asked her, "Have I ever really enjoyed my life? Seriously, in the last 15 years that we've known each other, have you ever witnessed me finding joy in the everyday moments of living?"

Her answer was a resounding "no."

She mentioned that I seemed to experience joy when I accomplished a big task or completed a challenging project. Other than that...no joy. Instead, my focus had been on performance, achievement, and success.

Creativity Unlocks the Mind

Many of us structure our daily life and work to eliminate as much guesswork as possible. We generally choose the same meals to prepare for our family over and over. We go to the same stores to shop week after week. We develop a method of carrying out our jobs day after day.

All of this is in an effort to reduce the number of decisions we need to make and create shortcuts to the end results we desire.

In the process, we end up creating deeply ingrained ruts that restrict how we carry out each of life's tasks. On one hand, it saves time and energy. On the other, the routine that once created convenience ultimately results in boredom, mindlessness, and a loss of heart. One day can rarely be distinguished from the next when our priority is found in greasing the rails of life in order to eradicate the possibility of change.

No only do we become stuck in our ways, but we eventually lack an ability to overcome unexpected challenges.

The nurturing of creativity unlocks the steering wheel of our minds and allows us to turn to the right and left...opening up new paths that have yet to be explored. By intentionally setting aside time to cultivate creativity, we're choosing to make space for new things to come into our minds (and ultimately our lives).

If you're sick and tired of your current life, there's no better time than the present to leverage creativity and allow a new normal to emerge. One of the reasons why you're in the situation you're in is probably because you thought the 'same way' was the best way. If you've been doing the same thing over and over expecting different results, most people would consider you insane.

That's why creativity is so critical.

You have an endless well of resources to draw upon in the process of creating the life you truly long for. It does require a level of intentionality, but once you begin to nurture it, you'll begin to see new opportunities opening up all around you...all because of creativity.

Playfulness Unlocks the Heart
While we structure the creativity right out of our lives, we dismiss playfulness as childish and immature. The essence of playfulness is an ability to experience a true freedom that allows for uninhibited amusement. Rather than allowing this sense of play to emerge from within ourselves, we often rely on outside forces (like alcohol) to release our inhibitions and propel us into a counterfeit experience of true recreation.

The smile and laughter of a child in the midst of play is the most powerful picture of playfulness we have. The freedom to experience the moment and the joy found in simple pleasures is evidence of a child's open heart. They're open to fully experiencing the world around them...taking it all in...not only with their eyes, but with their hearts.

As we grow up, many of us have developed a calloused heart in response to the pain and disappointment of life. We protect our hearts from further damage and ward off any experiences that may encroach on the boundaries we've put in place. This is why the arts, playfulness, and even spirituality are experiences we long for, but we avoid them due to the inherent need to open up the innermost part of who we are.

Many people I speak with who are in need of a life launch have sealed off their hearts from the rest of the world. They've been so beat down (either by life's circumstances or the results of their own poor decisions) that they just want the pain to stop. In some ways, you'd think that buckling down and getting even more serious would be the path to finding hope, healing, and a fresh start. While there is definitely a place for goals and timelines, a new sense of playfulness will rejuvenate your heart like nothing else.

Nurturing Your Soul Through Creativity and Play

As I was re-launching my life, I knew that I had to unlock my mind and heart through creativity and play. There was something missing, and I wanted to re-trace my path to find out where I last experienced it.

Through conversations with my wife (who I was still trying to reconcile with) and my own self-reflection, I realized that I eliminated most of these 'frivolous' activities mid-way through my college experience. After my sophomore year, I became engaged to Laura, continued on in my role as photo editor for the college yearbook and newspaper, became a teacher's assistant to my favorite professor, worked for Nabisco 20 hours a week, and set a goal of finishing my BA and MA in four years total. And I wonder why I quit experiencing creativity and playfulness!?!

Before this transition into 'success mode,' I remember that I enjoyed so many things…

> **Photography** – the creativity of capturing and developing the images in what's the now-defunct 'darkroom.'
>
> **Basketball** – the enjoyment of competition with friends without any thought of trying to 'make the team.'
>
> **Bodyboarding** – the freedom of the ocean and the exhilaration of catching one wave after another.
>
> **Painting** – the opportunity to express my vision through the medium of physical objects.
>
> **Exploring** – the adventure of finding a new place and enjoying whatever it has to offer.

I had not experienced most of these activities since I was 20 years old, but I remembered the way they made me feel. I remember the excitement of seeing a magical image appear from my camera, the pure enjoyment of slam-dunking a basketball, and the exhilaration of catching a wave. Yet, it had been much too long since I had experienced any of those things.

During those six months of living alone, I purchased a basketball and body board and began to enjoy both activities once again…minus the dunking part. I picked up some fresh art supplies, and I painted a piece called "Broken Promises" on a 3'x4' canvas. And, I started exploring new towns in our area…finding the gems that they each had to offer.

After I was welcomed back home a few months later, I bought a new digital SLR camera…my first camera in over 15 years. Without the need for film or an accompanying darkroom, I found myself enamored by the newfound digital technology and the creativity that was soon unleashed.

Although the activities in and of themselves were pleasurable, the resulting joy spilled over into the rest of my life. I felt more energized to engage in relationships, motivated to tackle my to-do list, and resourceful to overcome challenges.

If you want to nurture a sense of creativity and playfulness during your life launch, I'd encourage you to…

1. **Reflect on creative and playful activities you have enjoyed.**
   Think about the most creative seasons of your life. What were you're doing on a regular basis that nurtured your imagination? What were you listening to? What were you reading? What stirred up your emotions?

   Reflect on your childhood playfulness. Were there certain games, sports, and or activities that brought out the greatest sense of play within you? What did it feel like when you were playing?

2. Choose one creative/playful activity to try out this week.
By creative, I mean something that brings out the inner artist that's within you. Paint a painting, draw a drawing, create a scrapbook, decorate a room, or whatever it is that interests you. Also, choose another activity that's full of pleasure and enjoyment without the need to produce anything.

Don't commit to these activities for life. Just try them out a couple of times. When you first experience them, they'll feel a bit awkward, but try them again. Drag someone along with you if you need the support.

3. Be aware of how you feel before, during, and afterwards.
Were you nervous with anticipation? Did you enjoy the process – not focusing on the outcome? What about afterwards? Could you sense a difference in the rest of your life? Did you feel more alive in some way?

More than that end product (whatever it may be), my hope is that you experience a greater sense of being 'alive' as a creative, playful human being. There's something about doing something out of the norm that stretches your mind and heart. The energy gained by participating in these simple activities carries over into your job, friendships, and family.

I have to admit. I felt quite awkward 'trying on' some of these things. In some ways, I felt like a kid again...and I loved it. I pushed beyond the notion that other people may laugh at me, and I simply enjoyed the freedom of the moment.

One thing I was learning through my own life launch was that I could do whatever I wanted...however I wanted to do it. There was an emerging freedom that was intoxicating. The opinions of others didn't (and still don't) matter when it comes to me expressing my creativity and playfulness. Of course, I need to exercise responsibility so that I avoid causing pain or harm to someone else (which is difficult to do while painting), but my greatest sense is the unbelievable freedom that comes from nurturing creativity and playfulness in my life.

Creativity and Play: The Process of Intention

As we encounter each of The Seven Spheres of Transformation, I want to invite you to reflect on the questions in The Process of Intention. These questions are designed to help you be intentional about re-launching this area of your life.

1. Who am I?
As you think about creativity and play, who are you? If you believe that you were created by a Creator, do you have inherit abilities to create in this life? Were these qualities present within you as a child only to be done away with as you matured? Or, is it possible that they're part of your identity even now?

2. What do I want?
Do you really see the value of creativity and playfulness? What are the end results that you long for in your life? Do you want to have more freedom to express your thoughts and emotions? Would you want an energized life where you're not hindered by how other people have done things in the past?

3. What truths will keep me focused?
The dark voices seem to attack us at our places of greatest weakness. The arena of creativity is so fragile for many of us. We hear lies that people will make fun of us or it's not worthwhile or that we're not creative. Meanwhile, there are extraordinary amounts of creativity and playfulness within us…crying out to be released from our beings.

What's the truth about who you are? Let me tell you! You are creative. You have the ability to create amazing works of art… whether through visual arts, performance arts, interior design, fashion design, or any other form of self-expression. And, you have the opportunity to be playful and enjoy this life we've been generously given.

4. How will I take action?

Don't just think about being creative...do something! It doesn't matter what it is. Create anything...and show it to someone. In fact, give it to them as a gift. It's from your heart to theirs. Don't worry about what they'll think. Trust that your heart will shine through.

How will you be playful this week? What will you do that allows those inhibitions to melt away? Will you dance with your kids to crazy music in your living room? Will you go surfing again? How about picking up that tennis racket and dusting it off? Or, maybe you want to pull out that skateboard and take it for a spin.

5. Who will walk with me?

Finally, you will need someone to be creative and playful with. Who comes to mind? Perhaps someone who embodies these traits and you find them to be open to sharing their gifts with others. Not someone who's the most accomplished artist...I'm just talking about someone who has the freedom to creatively express himself or herself. Ask them to join with you in this new adventure.

The life you truly want is waiting for you. Are you going after it?

Physical Well-being
chapter 14

As my relationship with the 'other woman' escalated, my desire to modify my physical body intensified as well. If this woman was going to see me shirtless, I definitely didn't want to look the way I did. It's not as if I was obese, but I just didn't feel comfortable with my body.

I was 6'5" tall and 215 pounds...the heaviest I had ever been. My gut was protruding, and my man-boobs were in need of a training bra.

I hit the gym hard...running, lifting, and sweating off the pounds. I quit fast-food cold turkey, and I started to eat better and less. Within two weeks, I was fully committed to the 'affair and divorce' diet. I left my wife and 15 pounds in the dust.

After moving in with my wife's best friend, I kept working out to deal with the anxiety and stress of all the transition, and I ate enough Lean Cuisine frozen dinners to last me for the rest of my life. I was looking better than I had in years, and my energy level was increasing each day.

Fast-forward 40 days...
I was all alone...and I was working out even more.

I worked out in my own psych hospital room, and I kept working out once or twice a day when I moved into my new apartment. Frankly, the endorphins from the exercise were one of the things that saved my life.

By the time I moved back in with my family, I had lost 35 pounds... down to a lean 180. Let's just say that I didn't stay at that same fighting weight after I started eating my wife's amazing cooking once again.

The Body, Mind, and Soul Connection
During the 10 years I spent overworking, I was completely unaware of the toll that it was taking on my body and soul. I skipped breakfast for months (maybe even years) at a time, and I never thought twice about it. I'd eat a super-sized, fast food lunch almost every day of the week. That is, unless I forgot to eat lunch altogether, because I was too busy working away on an 'urgent' project. For dinner, I would regularly go back for seconds by dipping into the pots on the kitchen stove. To top things off, I'd often stuff my face with a Diet Dr. Pepper and handfuls of whatever I could find...cookies, chips, crackers, and even raw hot dogs...right before bedtime.

It was a vicious cycle of unintended starvation and binging. Anytime I felt down, overwhelmed, or anxious, I'd turn to caffeine, sugar, and fried food. Then, I'd work some more, and completely forget to eat.

Although I rarely got sick, it wasn't until I stopped the overworking that I realized how messed up my body really was. I was a 35 year old, pudgy mound of tiredness. The connection between my physical well-being, the functionality of my brain, and the processing of my emotions was finally starting to register.

You'd think that a grown man would understand the implications, but I guess I thought I was somehow super-human. I thought I could feed my body whatever I craved, and it wouldn't impact my thoughts or feelings. I assumed that I could keep working day after day with little or no rest and think it would never have much of an effect on my ability to communicate clearly. I somehow thought that I could carry the emotional and spiritual weight of the non-profit I founded, and it wouldn't have repercussions on my physical health.

By looking at the obesity rates in the United States, I'm wondering if most people are thinking the same thing. As a culture, we seem to believe we're special...not needing to heed the natural ways in which we're constructed as human beings.

We are not machines.

Our bodies, minds, and souls are interconnected in ways that require us to take care of ourselves. That's probably one of the reasons why you even picked up this book. Your body isn't looking or feeling or working the way in which it used to...or the way you'd like it to.

It's not too late. You can do something about it. You can learn from some of my mistakes and join me in choosing a new kind of life.

Six Things I Learned After Ten Years of Overworking

Although my original motives for getting into shape were quite skewed, I was starting to feel the positive results of creating a new normal. I was also realizing the repercussions of mistreating my body for years. See if any of these learnings resonate with you...

1. Eat crap, and you'll feel like it, too.
I'm not a big fan of sweets, but I regularly ate super-sized burgers, fries, and sodas that would make any grown man's gut start to bulge. I ate that way for so long I thought the bloated feeling with the accompanying sluggishness was normal. Once I cut out fast food and began eating smaller portions, I felt more energetic and my body started shaping up.

2. Don't move your body, and your mind will become mush.
I semi-prided myself on not exercising or doing anything in the outdoors. I thought my mind could function just fine in the dimly-lit, unnaturally-cooled space called an 'office'. Once my life imploded, I found myself venturing to the beach and area parks on a regular basis. I needed the spiritual stimulation, but I also found my body responding positively. I continued to exercise regularly, and my mind was gaining greater clarity and an ability to process

possible changes in my life.

3. Sleep a little and rest even less, and you'll feel tired…duh.

Although I tended to get eight hours of sleep, I rarely took a complete day off from work. If I wasn't physically at my office, I probably had my laptop open on the couch. And, if I wasn't looking at email or researching something on the web, my mind was incessantly processing things I was concerned about.

The lack of rest made me continually tired.
Can you believe it?

In retrospect, I realize what an idiot I was. Of course, you can see my foolish behavior, but can you see your own? I'm not alone in believing that I'm super-human. Most likely, you have been making choices that are negatively impacting your physical wellbeing. Are you getting enough sleep and rest? Or, do you think you can keep 'going and going' forever?

4. Don't care for your brain, and people will quit liking you.

More than any other component of my physical well being, I completely underestimated the impact of brain health. I never even knew that my brain could be unhealthy. As I mentioned earlier, I was introduced to a book called "Change Your Brain, Change Your Life" by Dr. Daniel Amen, and I was given the opportunity to receive a brain scan by the Amen Clinic in Newport Beach, CA. I knew a friend who had great success with this process so I went ahead with it…although I was quite nervous.

I was scared to death that they were going to say that I had 'axe-murderer' tendencies! Thankfully, I didn't…and still don't as far as I know.

They perform a scan to determine the various activity levels of your brain…checking to see if there is under or over-activity. In the end, I was encouraged to try a mild dose of an anti-anxiety medication to decrease the level of activity in my basal ganglia…

controlling our 'fight or flight' responses. The results were tremendous. In fact, I can't believe I thought the ongoing 'buzz' in my brain was actually normal. I can truly be present in relationships like never before.

Prior to the brain scan and ongoing medication, I found myself impatient with people around me and more focused on projects than anything else. Although that is my natural tendency (and strength), my mind is not consumed with the to-do list inside my brain anymore. I can be connecting and empathetic without the need to be busy constantly.

5. Work as long as you can, and you'll become unproductive.
I believed the lie that I would be even more productive if I just worked harder and longer. What I didn't realize was that not only do you become unproductive after 60 or so hours a week, but you really lose productivity after expending that much mental and physical energy for months and even years at a time.

I would lose track of my thoughts, and it would take me hours to prepare projects. I would find myself getting easily distracted by anything and everything other than that which I was supposed to be working on. All this was a result of working too hard for too long. It became the norm, and I found myself having to work even more hours just to keep up with what I started.

6. Combine all of the above, and you'll eventually burn out.
It would never happen to me...or at least that's what I thought. In many ways, I thought I was invincible and above the natural laws of the human body. I prided myself in working harder than anyone else around.

Eventually, it all took its toll, and I burned out.

I didn't care anymore. I just wanted out, and my body was begging for rest and rejuvenation. Although I was twitching from the loss of my drug (work), my mind was finally slowing down in the weeks after I resigned from my leadership role at the non-profit I founded. I was finally done...burnt to a crisp.

Creating a 'New Normal' for Your Body

I knew I had to make some serious changes if I was going to get healthy again. Frankly, I'm not sure I ever was healthy. Maybe, I just needed to get healthy for the first time.

The crazy thing was that my physical well-being wasn't even one of the top priorities during my life launch. Although I wasn't happy with the way my body looked, my main focus was on trying to win back my wife and kids and reconstruct my relationships. What I found out along the way was that the condition of my physical body was inextricably tied to every other part of my life.

Frankly, that's one of the biggest learnings I hope you carry away from this book. To truly experience a re-launching of your life, you will be most effective if you're willing to examine every aspect of your life... including your physical well-being. I want to invite you to take a few moments to reflect on the questions I began asking myself...

1. Food - What do I *need* to eat and drink to be healthy?

There are a million diets on the market that will tell you the best way to be healthy, lose weight, and experience maximum performance. I don't care what you do, but you've got to find something that works for you. I'm not suggesting you go on a diet.

I'm strongly encouraging you to create a 'new normal' when it comes to food intake.

Maybe you need to keep a food journal for an entire week to increase your awareness of what you're putting in your body. Do you really want to put all those processed, sugar-infused, deep-fried foods in your system? I will be honest and tell you that I struggle with this. I love to eat crap! It tastes great, but it doesn't make me feel (or look) great.

If you think about the creation of your human body, what do you think it was intended to consume in order to grow and thrive on this earth? If you don't want to thrive in this life, eat whatever you want. But, if you're looking to re-launch your life, start thinking about making different food choices...now.

2. Exercise - How can I move my body regularly to get fit?

Notice that I didn't use the word 'exercise' in the question. That's a dirty word for some of us. It's boring, sweat-producing, and takes time. I don't like to exercise. That's why I'm re-branding it as 'moving my body.' I don't mind doing that, and I just need to find all sorts of ways to keep moving my body so that I get fit *and* stay fit.

My 'old normal' position was on the couch with my laptop open. My 'new normal' position is up and moving...at least more than I used to. Once again, this is a struggle for me, but I'm heading in the right direction.

What physical activities can you find that you'll enjoy? Biking, walking the dog, running on the beach, surfing, kayaking, or maybe it is going to the gym. Whatever it is...it's all about a 'new normal.' It's not about getting on a kick where you're ready to become a workout fiend overnight. It can be as simple as putting on your tennis shoes and going for an evening walk with your spouse or a friend. It's all about creating a new way you're going to use your body on a daily basis.

3. Rest and Sleep - How much will I sleep and rest daily?

Once you determine how many hours of sleep you need to function at an optimal level, then you'll need to determine how to structure your life accordingly. That's where the problem comes in for most of us.

We know that we need 7-9 hours of sleep depending on our personal makeup. The question is...why do we stay up so late and get up so early? We're cheating our own bodies of the rest we need in order to create the kind of output we truly want. If you want to get great grades, perform in the workplace, and develop life-giving relationships, not getting a sufficient amount of sleep is the worst way to begin.

In the same way that we plan much of our lives, we need to plan our sleep. If you set a normal time to go to bed and a normal time to wake up, it will change your life.

4. Brain Health - What do I need to be clear and creative?
You may not have the financial wherewithal to get a brain scan, but you can begin to do some research on what your brain needs to function at a high level. Sleep is a great start. So is eating vegetables, nuts, and the all-important omega-3 fatty acids found in halibut, mackerel, salmon, trout and tuna. How about brain-healthy vitamins like vitamin E, C, and B12?

Beyond sleep and food, studies have shown that meditation and prayer are helpful forms of rehabilitation when it comes to brain health. Whether you're a person of faith or not, you may consider taking time to close your eyes and quiet your mind each day… reflecting on what you're thankful for. This simple meditation can rejuvenate your entire being.

Although this may go without saying, the old commercial that shows your 'brain on drugs' (eggs sizzling in a frying pan) is best to keep in mind. Tobacco, drugs, and even caffeine have an adverse affect on brain health, and they are to be avoided.

5. Work Hours - How can I structure work effectively?
I assumed that I could allow work to bleed over into every moment of my life and still remain effective and efficient. It just wasn't true for me, and it's not true for you either. It's a lie…a dark voice that seeks to destroy you.

If you're prone to workaholism like I am, you'll probably need the eyes and ears of a close friend or spouse to help you examine this part of your life. Unless you have an hourly job where you work 8am-5pm every day, it's unrealistic to think that work can be structured in a cut and dry fashion on a weekly basis. I know countless men and women who are in the corporate world, entertainment industry, and the non-profit arena...all of which have to find a rhythm that works best for them.

Frankly, I don't believe in balance much at all. I find that I'm out of balance on a regular basis. Because of my flexible life, I am spending a great deal of time with my family on some occasions, and there are other seasons when I'm very focused on a particular project. I think words like rhythm, new normal, and tension work well as I'm trying to constantly negotiate how I integrate work into my life...not life into my work.

6. Unhealthy Substances - What do I need to abstain from?
Okay, so you've got a dirty little secret, huh? What are you addicted to? Chocolate, caffeine, nicotine, weed? What is it? You may be the only person who knows what it is. If there's something that you're using as a coping mechanism to get you through your day, it's probably unhealthy. What would it look like to find the help you need in order to get to a place of health?

Are you overwhelmed after reflecting on those six categories? I am! Sheesh! The funny thing is that none of this is new to you. In fact, you may have skipped through this section, because it's all old news that you've been reading in magazines and hearing about on TV. It's nothing revolutionary at all.

What is revolutionary is the choice to be intentional about putting what you know into action!

Until you get serious about your physical well-being, it will continue to negatively impact every other aspect of your life. If you're overweight, it will impact your ability to enjoy a life-long relationship with your spouse and kids. If you're eating unhealthy foods and not exercising, it may result in heart disease and even cancer. If you're not paying attention to your sleep habits, rest periods, and the health of your brain, I guarantee you that your relationships are suffering. What are you going to do about it?

Take this unique season of life to re-launch your physical well-being. You can do it…and it'll be worth it.

Physical Well-Being: The Process of Intention

As we encounter each of The Seven Spheres of Transformation, I want to invite you to reflect on the questions in The Process of Intention. These questions are designed to help you be intentional about re-launching this area of your life.

1. **Who am I?**

   As you think about your physical well-being, who are you? I believe this body that we've been given is a gift from God. What if you began to see yourself as a gift? Not just your talents, strengths, and abilities. What if you actually saw the physical 'earth suit' you've been given as a gift for you to enjoy and take care of?

2. **What do I want?**

   What type of condition do you long for your physical well-being to be in? I'm not talking about the unrealistic thoughts of looking like that supermodel on the front of the magazine at the checkout stand. I mean…how do you want to feel? What do you want to experience in this life with and through your physical body? If you can't be clear about what you want, you'll never be able to experience it.

3. **What truths will keep me focused?**

   Have you heard dark voices when it comes to your body? "You're too fat. You'll never feel good. There's no way that your body will ever work right." Heard anything like that before? I have. So, what's the truth?

   How about…"I was created with an amazing, powerful, and beautiful body. It was given to me as a gift. I will treat it as a gift, and it will respond positively. I'm thankful for what I've been given." If you really believed those truths, what difference do you think it would make in your life?

4. How will I take action?
If you don't do something about your physical well-being, nothing will change. Actually, let me take that back. It will probably get worse! You know what you need to do. Now, make a plan.

Sign up for a gym membership, and go. Get a notepad, and start an eating journal. Schedule when you'll wake up and when you'll go to sleep. Start treating your brain in a healthy way…pray, meditate, and eat healthy foods. Get help for the substances that you're abusing. Set a timeline and get going. It's worth the effort. It takes time, but you will see results!

5. Who will walk with me?
Last but not least…who are you going to walk with? Like no other area of your life launch, physical well-being is extremely improved by your willingness to partner with someone else who has the same desires.

Find a walking buddy, share your eating plan, and be honest when you stumble. You won't do this perfectly or get it right all the time. You're going to starve and binge. You're going to be sedentary once in awhile. The question is…are you moving forward? Your ability to take ground is directly connected to your willingness to find someone to get healthy with.

Spirituality
chapter 15

I've never stopped sensing God's presence…not even in the moments when I was leaving my wife and running as fast as I could into the arms of another woman. It's not as if I felt God's approval…just a continual loving Presence.

My therapist seemed to think that God draws even closer to us when we're blowing it, because we need Love in those moments more than any other time. It's funny how others who speak for God suggest a departure in some sense. It's as if the mere presence of Almighty somehow brings approval of our unhealthy and even destructive actions.

Presence doesn't equal approval.
Presence equals Love.

What you may or may not know is that the non-profit I founded was actually a *church*. Yes…for over 10 years, I was a pastor of a Christian church where I sought to help people awaken to a rich, meaningful life by following Jesus.

In the meantime, I was working myself to death…trying to somehow bolster my identity and become 'somebody.' You can imagine the negative reaction from those in the congregation who had trusted me, embraced my teachings, and followed my lead. They were less than thrilled about my decision to leave my wife and resign as the pastor of the church I had founded.

Yet, God did not leave me...at least I didn't sense that to be the case. Hurt and angry people said that I was evil, and they demonized me by seeing the negative in everything I did (or had done). Ultimately, they questioned the authenticity of my words for all those years, and many of them viciously attacked me as they were fueled with venom and self-righteousness.

I don't blame them. When we're in pain and are confronted with disappointment, we oftentimes lash out in anger rather than grieving the loss of expectations.

The loss of my marriage, my role as a pastor, and then my mistress caused me to deconstruct my spirituality over the course of two tumultuous years. It was during the re-launching of my life that I came to grips with how I was longing to live a great life, but I was tweaked in the trajectory of my heart.

I grew up in a Christian family, and 'church' in its various forms has been at the center of my existence. My father is a pastor, my mother is a 'pastor' although she doesn't have the title, and I ultimately became a pastor. I didn't plan for things to turn out that way, but there was a strong Nudge I couldn't resist. All that's to say, spirituality has been a major part of my upbringing, education, and vocation.

You may not believe in God or even be interested in a High Power. Chances are you believe in Something, but you're just not that sure how it all fits together.

Frankly, I'm not either.

All I know is that there is a real God who has deeply impacted my life, and 'Spirituality' is one of The Seven Spheres of Transformation that you'll want to address during your life launch.

Let me make things clear.
I'm not pushing my beliefs on you...
I just want to tell you about my own journey.

In no way is this an effort to get you to believe what I believe. I've quit that game. I'm more interested in provoking you to think deeply about your own spirituality and how it is impacting the whole of your life.

Connecting With God

My first memories of my spirituality were experienced in the living rooms of family friends. As part of a house church movement in the 1970s and 80s, we would gather on Sunday morning at someone's home, and the adults would sing, pray, and listen to a message from the Bible as the kids made handprints in the shag carpet. I didn't necessarily sense God's presence in a remarkable way, but it was obvious that my parents were experiencing something profound.

I was most enamored by the closeness of the relationships my parents developed with the other couples in the church. We would spend time at one another's homes, and there was a great sense of care and connection among these individuals. They were the closest of friends, and God seemed to have something to do with it.

As an adolescent, I prayed a prayer to ask Jesus into my heart, and I was baptized...a beginning step in most Christian churches. Beyond that, not much more happened. I picked up on all the things that my family was against like Halloween, the Easter bunny, secular music, and sex before marriage. Although I'm sure my parents were 'for' many things...I didn't pick up on those until much later in life.

In 1989, we moved from Kentucky to California, and we finally got involved in a 'normal' church...ya know...one with a church building.

As we started to attend the new church in Lodi, kids from the youth group would beg me to come to their event every week. What they didn't realize is that I was too cool for that. I was a photographer, and I was on the basketball team. They were just lame kids carrying their pleather-covered Bibles to youth group every week while cool kids were out doing something fun...which would be pretty much anything other than church.

I finally relented one Tuesday night, and I showed up. I drove my cream-colored station wagon into the church parking lot, and I nervously headed into the building. Within minutes, I found myself getting sucked into a frenetic game of 'capture the flag'...otherwise known as 'chase the cute girls.'

Within a couple of weeks, I was attending every Tuesday night, and I quickly noticed something different about these kids...especially two guys named Brian and Damon. They were seniors, and they were passionate about 'Jeeesuuus' as they called him. They did stuff that I hadn't ever thought of...like they read the Bible and prayed in 'tongues' (a crazy-sounding language that's supposed to be just between you and God) and raised their hands while we sang songs. Weird stuff for sure!

One February evening, the youth pastor invited anyone up front who wanted to follow 'Jeeesuuus', and he started praying for everyone. As my heart began pounding out of my chest, I knew he was talking to me. Sure, I had grown up in a Christian home, been baptized, and followed all the 'rules'...but this was different.

I went up front, and Brian and Damon were there to pray for people. I looked at the pastor and said, "I want something different. I want what they have."

Tears began to stream down my pimply face, and I felt like something had changed that evening. I felt something...God, I think. Although I was a pretty straight and narrow kid, I liked this whole idea of 'living for Jesus' and helping others experience that, too...but I was a bit overzealous to say the least.

I started wearing Jesus shirts to school including the one with Buddha on a cross and some sort of "your god didn't die for you" phrase emblazoned on the front. With my Bible in hand and cross around my neck, I

Spirituality

was making looooots of friends.

Within the next year, I found myself on a plane with 15 or so other kids heading to Dallas, Texas for a youth convention. The climax of the multi-day event was a giant 10,000 kid 'church meeting' in the convention center to ring in the new year...1991.

At the beginning of the conference, I noticed a fresh-out-of-bible-college 'salesman' who would stand at the front door and pass out literature trying to get kids to come to their school. Since I had already been accepted into the photojournalism department at Western Kentucky University, I had no interest whatsoever in some un-accredited bible college.

Day after day, we would enter the doors, and I'd notice the same guy over and over. By the end of the three days, my ears were filled with the speakers' words, and my heart was overflowing with questions about the future. I started to wonder if a bible college was for me.

On the final evening, it was like a replay from that night a year before at my church's youth group. The pastor asked us if we were committed to 'go' anywhere God wanted us to go. If we were, he invited us to come down to the floor of the convention center to be prayed for. As more and more kids streamed down the stairs, I found my legs moving toward the aisle. It was as if my heart had bypassed my head, and I was going down to that floor whether I liked it or not.

As I kneeled on the ice-cold, concrete floor of the giant convention center with hundreds of other sweaty, puberty-induced teenagers, I knew what He was calling me to do.

I knew that I wasn't supposed to go back to Kentucky. I knew that I wasn't supposed to be a Sports Illustrated photographer like I thought.

God was calling me to be a...*pastor.*

I knew it deep within. I didn't tell anyone that night, but I knew it...and that's all that mattered.

As I walked in the door to my home, I dropped my bags, and my parents asked the obligatory question, "How was the trip?"

"Fine," I muttered as I moped down the hallway.

After a few minutes, I emerged from my room and plopped down on the living room couch. I could feel the tears starting to well up in nervous anticipation of my parent's reaction. I did my best to suck the salty drops back in, but it didn't work. With sniffling and snorting between each word, I blubbered through it..."I don't think...I'm supposed to... go back to Kentucky...I think I'm supposed to be a...pastor."

With tears streaming down my face, my parents started to laugh.

"What? Why are you laughing at me?" I asked in confusion.

"We thought this might be where your life would take you, but we didn't want to push you in to something," my dad reassured. I began to see my parents eyes fill with understanding.

My First Try at Spirituality

After four years of college and a three year stint in the corporate world, I finally entered full-time ministry as a pastor. Ten years later, I was burned out, and I couldn't figure out how to re-launch my life without looking like a total fool. Rather than humbly admitting that I was in need of some serious retooling, I chose to implode everything through a very public affair.

As I recovered from this mess, I was able to deconstruct a great deal of what I had been experiencing over the previous 10 years. Here's what I began to see about the spirituality I had developed...

1. God became a product I sold.

While starting a new church, it can be extremely difficult to rally a sufficient amount of people to create momentum and ultimately pay the bills that go along with the venture...including my own salary. I gave in to the temptation to help God develop a more appealing persona by creating a slick and sexy package.

There are an abundance of tools available to pastors to attract potential church attenders...fancy lighting, booming sound systems, ginormous video screens, and eye-catching graphics. We used every bit of it...all in an effort to help people connect with God.

Hundreds were positively impacted, and countless lives were changed. Marriages were healed, and addictions were left in the dust. Meanwhile, I was coming up with every possible way to prop Jesus up and make him look more sexy so that even more people would come and worship him.

During the two years of re-launching my own life, I clearly saw that I had made God into not much more than a slickly packaged product...and I was sick of it. I wanted God to be God...not a product I had to hawk at a makeshift flea market every Sunday.

2. I connected with God so I could teach others.
Rather than creating an awareness of God in my life so that my soul would be fed and my attitudes and actions would be transformed, I was more interested in coming up with something powerful I could teach others. With Sunday morning rolling around every seven days, creating an entertaining, life-changing message was more important than nurturing my own relationship with the One who created me.

After leaving ministry, I realized that there was no reason to read the Bible, because I wasn't going to be giving a Sunday message. There was no real reason to spend time meditating and praying, because I wasn't trying to be inspired to pump people up. In reality, I had very little need for God.

3. My life was more focused on 'doing' rather than 'being.'
Because my full-time job was to lead a church, I was consumed with thinking of projects I could enroll others in. Whether it was a mid-week group to study the Bible or a multi-thousand person

event to impact the city...my focus was on performance.

I was a driven leader that coerced my staff and hundreds of volunteers to perform with excellence and efficiency...all in the name of reaching out to our community with a message of Hope and Love. There was very little time or space in my spirituality for 'being.' In its very essence, 'being' is the process of simply existing in the presence of God. In this space, peace, hope, and transformation begin to develop. It's more an attitude than an action... more a way of the heart.

4. Doing good things for God was my total focus.

There is a passage in the ancient scriptures that warns us about growing "weary in well doing." That was me. I had such a deep desire to make a positive impact on the world that I didn't stop to ask myself what was driving all of this energy. And, I definitely didn't consider the negative ramifications upon my own health. Good deeds were more of the focus than God's desires for my family and my life.

5. I didn't take the concept of Sabbath (or rest) seriously.

The last thing that became crystal clear as I deconstructed my spirituality was the lack of attention to what's called the Sabbath. In the Bible, God instructed the Jews to set aside one day a week for rest. Although this is widely understood in Christian churches, it isn't widely practiced.

Frankly, I rarely took a day off, and when I did, I was still thinking about work. Somehow, I thought God would reward this, and I thought the church would benefit in the process. Not so much.

These learnings are obviously very specific to my life and journey of deconstruction. How about your own life? As you hear me process what I've experienced, what comes up in your own mind?

When were you first aware of God's existence/presence in your life? Who did you learn from, and what were your early experiences like?

How has spirituality played a daily role in your life up to this point?

Are there assumptions or ways of connecting with God that have been detrimental or harmful to you? Are there beliefs that you need to revisit? Are there attitudes you'd like to adjust? Are there behaviors that aren't aligning with who you want to be?

Spirituality...Take Two
As I lived alone and then ultimately moved back in with my family, I was slowly making changes to my spirituality. As I deconstructed certain parts, I allowed the rubble of what used to be to simply lie there. I wasn't in a hurry to find all the answers or put something back together.

You may find yourself in a place where you're feeling disconnected, resentful, angry, or bitter. Don't give up on God or the people who represent God (in whatever faith you've been part of). If you leave spirituality out of your life and ignore it, you'll be missing a key component to your life launch. If you don't actively and intentionally engage who God is and what God is doing in your life, you'll lack the tremendous power that your launch can have otherwise.

As I started reconstructing my faith, here are the things that started to truly come together for me. Once again, this is *my* journey...not yours. I'm not trying to propose my spirituality for your life. I share this simply for the purpose of challenging you to think about your own connection with God and what that means to you.

   1. God loves me and never leaves me - no matter what you say.
   I blew it big time! I left my wife and kids and resigned as the pastor of a church in order to have an affair. It was horrible...and yet, God loves me. In my faith, the Bible is central to my knowledge and understanding of who God is. The ancient scriptures tell me that God will never leave me nor forsake me. God is with me no matter what.

   Although some people may try to convince me that I'm tarnished in the eyes of God, I just don't buy it. I'm a sinful human being, and I'm forgiven by God because of Jesus' death on the cross some 2,000 years ago.

Once again, this is stuff that's important in my spirituality. You've got to figure out who God is for you and lean into that faith.

2. Jesus seems to know how to live a rich, meaningful life.
As I re-read the gospels (four stories of Jesus' life and ministry), I was convinced that Jesus seemed to have a good handle on how to live an amazing life. Up until 2.5 years ago, I was living a frantic, hurried, stress-filled life. I wasn't living the life of hope, joy, peace, and love that I saw Jesus living. I wasn't experiencing what he taught about, and I knew that something had to change.

Instead of being consumed by doing all sorts of good stuff for God, what if I just started following Jesus? In the Bible, Jesus called all his disciples with two words…"Follow me!" That's it. He challenged them to leave everything else behind and join him on the journey. So, I'm trying that perspective out now. What if I just learned from the teachings of Jesus and followed him?

3. I'm out of the sales business - I model, share, & encourage.
Full-time church work feels like a sales business to me. Maybe it's not for other people, but it's a brutal field to be in. Ironically, I feel just as 'called' as ever to help people connect with God and live an amazing life, but I don't ever want to 'sell' God again.

For me, selling God looks like creating a slick package to make God look attractive to people who wouldn't otherwise be interested. I just can't do it anymore. I'm not knocking it for other pastors and leaders, but my weaknesses get triggered too easily by orchestrating a big weekly hoopla to praise Jesus.

At this point, I just want to model a life of following Jesus authentically. I'm focused on sharing my learnings along the way with anyone who is interested in listening. And, finally, I'm passionate about encouraging people who are trying to love and follow after

God themselves.

Model, share, and encourage...feels much more natural than package, promote, and proselytize.

4. People are more important than anything else in this life.
I love projects. I love envisioning, strategizing, and executing a plan that results in the accomplishment of a goal. There's something powerful and adrenaline-producing about that experience. Unfortunately, much of the reason why I focused so much on building a church in the past was a deep desire to reinforce my own identity. I was more concerned about the hit of adrenaline and the boost to my ego than I was about the people involved.

With the help of some anxiety-reducing meds and the retooling of my heart, I've chosen for people to be the most important thing in my life. Not so I can leverage them to accomplish my goal... but so I can partner with them to see their vision come to fruition.

More than ever before, I love spending time with people (despite the fact that I'm a slight introvert). It is my belief that God created every single one of us uniquely, and we are made in God's image. There is something extraordinary about human beings, and every person deserves love, care, and compassion. This is as much part of my spirituality as anything else.

5. Rest, playfulness, and creativity seem important, too.
Although I've touched base on these topics in previous chapters, I believe they truly flow out of my relationship with God. They aren't disconnected from who God is. In fact, these three things flow out of who God created me to be.

Rest is something that God commands me to do, and I'm learning to embrace God's directive. It is for my own benefit, and it is a spiritual practice. Playfulness is an outgrowth of my ability to enjoy life moment by moment. If God gave me this one and only life to live, I want to playfully enjoy it. Finally, I want to express the creativity within me. If God is my Creator, I believe that God put the ability to create within me. I don't have to be the best artist in the world in order to express these unbelievable gifts.

I want 'Spirituality' to be a daily part of my life...just like the other six Spheres of Transformation. I don't want my faith in God to be limited to a particular time or place. I want total life integration in the same way that the other parts of my life launch are interconnected. Remember, we live holistic lives where every part of us impacts the rest of us.

Spirituality: The Process of Intention

As we have encountered each of The Seven Spheres of Transformation, I have invited you to reflect on the questions in The Process of Intention. These questions are designed to help you be intentional about re-launching this area of your life.

1. Who am I?

As you think about your spirituality, who are you? Are you just another face that will exist 70-100 years on this earth...or are you more than that? Have you been created by a Higher Power? Is there something unique about your being that goes beyond a physical body? Do you have a body that happens to have a spirit? Or, are you a spirit that is encased within a body? Who are you?

2. What do I want?

When it comes to your faith, what do you want? Do you want a relationship with God that is life-giving? Do you think God is out to squash all your fun and knock some sense into you if you get out of line? Is that really what you want in terms of spirituality?

Do you want more peace in your life? How about joy...do you have enough of that? What about love? Do you want to receive and give more love on a daily basis? How about your values? Are you living a life you're proud of? Do you enjoy the results that you're getting? Get clear about the spirituality you long for.

3. What truths will keep me focused?

Now that you're getting clear, the dark voices won't be far behind. "God couldn't love a person like you. Don't even bother with spirituality…it's a sham. If you can't see it, don't believe it." Have you heard those voices before? I have. Fight back with what you know to be true. What are the truths that have been placed deep within your heart that you need to call upon as you take steps in your new spiritual journey? Take hold of them and don't let go.

4. How will I take action?

Here's where the rubber hits the road. What actions do you want to take this week? Perhaps, you'd like to purchase a few books to explore some new aspects of your faith. Maybe it's time for you to gather with others who hold your same faith. Or, more likely, you don't even have a place to gather with others. Maybe your action step is to talk with a close friend about their faith and ask them some questions.

It may also serve you well to begin setting aside some time each day or week to cultivate a greater awareness of God in your life. Slow down. Breathe deeply. Talk to God. Ask for wisdom, and I bet Wisdom will start showing up.

5. Who will walk with me?

Finally, who are you going to trust to walk with you on this journey? It's probably going to be someone you admire. Who is that person who is peaceful, loving, and overflowing with good deeds? Who seems to be living out their faith in a way that attracts you?

Here's an idea…what if you asked them out to lunch? What if you spent time just asking them questions and listening to their heart? I said 'heart' not just their 'head.' Yes, their answers will be important, but truly listening to what's going on in that person's heart will tell you a great deal about how they integrate their faith into their life. I bet God has placed someone in your life that is ready, willing, and able to begin walking with you.

Head Up, Shoulders Back, One Step Forward
chapter 16

After being released from the psych hospital, I was dropped off at my apartment by a friend. I pulled out my cell phone to check for any voicemails, and it turned out that my divorce attorney had been trying to get a hold of me for the last two days to share the good news.

My wife was taking me to court to gain temporary custody of the kids. My meltdown in front of my son while I was with him was the primary impetus, but the subsequent hospital visit for three days didn't exactly help.

"May I speak with Scott Jarvis, please?"

"Yes, one moment," the receptionist said.

"This is Scott Jarvis. May I help you?"

"Scott, it's David Trotter. You've been trying to get a hold of me?"

"Yeah, where have you been?"

"Uh…I've…I've been in the hospital for three days."

"We have to know these things. You need to keep us informed about anything that would affect your case."

Seriously? This guy is scolding me for not calling him while I'm in a psych hospital. He's obviously never been through the hell I have.

It turned out that we had a court appointment on Friday where the judge could give my wife full, temporary custody of the kids. My attorney's plan was to work toward an agreement outside of the courtroom.

Friday arrived, and I slipped on my dress slacks that were now hanging off me like my big brother's clothes. The 'affair and divorce diet' was really working now.

I walked into the giant hallway of the county courthouse to see my wife and two of our friends sitting with her on a bench. As Laura looked away, I stared at all three of them with vengeance in my heart. Although I was glad that Laura had their support, it also felt like I was left all alone to fend for myself. I headed straight toward my one ally, my attorney, for last minute preparations.

"David, I've already spoken with your wife's attorney, and I think we can come to an agreement outside the court room. How do you feel about…" He was interrupted by the presence of my wife's attorney as she walked up.

"Have you explained the options to your client yet?" she butted in.

"We were just getting ready to go over those now," he responded kindly.

"Well, he needs to know that…" She continued on until I was sick of listening.

"Get this lady out of here." I said it right in front of her…I didn't care. "I don't have to listen to this crap. She's not my attorney."

He shooed her away, and we discussed my option. There weren't really options on the table. There was only *one* option.

Either I get to see the kids three times a week for three hours each time with a chaperone...or she planned to go into the courtroom and fight for temporary custody.

I opted for three times a week, and we arranged for three of our friends to be the chaperones by making a few calls on the spot. The utter humiliation of being followed around by a personal friend while I spend time with my own children would be worth it. I didn't care. I just wanted to salvage my relationship with the two most precious people on the planet.

Within the next two weeks, I found myself addressing a second legal issue...a request for a restraining order by the husband of my mistress. After melting down in front of my son, I dropped him off with a family friend at my former church. I headed straight to the home of the woman who just left me, and I wanted to speak with her.

I knocked at her door, yelled her name, and looked in the garage window to see if her car was there...all things her neighbors reported to her husband.

Frankly, I had no intentions of ever being in contact with her again after I got out of the hospital, but her husband didn't want to take any chances.

This was a great start to re-launching my life! Geez.

I called my attorney, and he delivered the bad news that he couldn't assist me in defending myself...my mistress and I had retained his services for both of our divorces. Therefore, it would be a conflict of interest!

With only a couple of days until the court appearance, I didn't have time to find another attorney nor did I want to spend the money. I figured I could fight the restraining order on my own. The last thing I wanted was the judge in my custody dispute catching a glimpse of a restraining order on my record.

I was committed to beating this thing on my own…no matter what.

According to the paperwork and my research, I needed to prove why I was not a threat to their family. In my mind, the best way to prove that was through overwhelming evidence that our relationship was two-sided and that I was not interested in any further contact.

I spent 8 hours typing up complete documentation of our relationship from beginning to end, and I even got certified letters from the hospital psychiatrist and my therapist that I was no threat to their family. 24 hours before the case was to go to court, I received a call from the husband's attorney. They dropped everything, and I breathed a deep sigh of relief.

Within two months, I left my wife, wrecked my kids, ruined my career, hurt hundreds of people at the church I founded, almost committed suicide, and dealt with a custody dispute and the request for a restraining order.

This wasn't exactly what I had in mind when I made the decision re-launch my life.

I was envisioning a new intimate, romantic relationship with an adventurous life…combining my two kids with her four…making it all work…happily ever after.

It didn't quite work out that way.
In fact, it turned out even better!

Keeping Your Head Up

I had no clue how everything was going to unfold, but I knew that I had to keep my head up…something I remember my dad telling me to do on many occasions. Whether it was a strikeout at the plate or disappointing performance on the court, my head would hang toward the ground.

"Keep your head up, David," I remember my dad saying. "Things will get better…you just gotta stick with it."

Head Up, Shoulders Back, and One Step Forward

There's something powerful about keeping your head up in moments of adversity or even total loss. It can change your attitude, the condition of your heart, and even the countenance of your body. If you wait until you feel like holding your head up, you may miss out on opportunities that you need to take hold of during your life launch.

I'm well aware of the pain and loss associated with a broken life. The natural response to such disappointment is sadness and even depression. Frankly, if you're going through a dark season in your life, I would strongly encourage you to seek out a therapist or medical doctor and inquire about anti-depressant medication. My wife and I both used meds during this horrendous time in our lives, and I'm so thankful for the medical professionals who assisted us both.

Realistically though...medication isn't a magical pill that takes away all the pain and makes everything better. You and I have an opportunity to use the five questions in The Process of Intention in order to see radical change in The Seven Spheres of Transformation.

If you want to see profound change in your life, you'll need to make intentional choices on a daily basis. In the process, I'm encouraging you to 'keep your head up' which allows you to...

1. Choose to be tenacious.
The essence of 'keeping your head up' is tenacity. It's a 'I'm-never-gonna-give-up' attitude that compels you to keep going. As you re-launch your life, there will be good days and tough days, but a commitment to your own health and transformation is key.

Frankly, there were times when I just wanted to call it quits and end my life, but I saw the faces of my children. I didn't want them to have a legacy of suicide, and I wanted them to have a healthy father to love them as they continued to succeed in life.

There were other times in which I just wanted to quit seeking a rich, meaningful life. I thought it would just be easier to give up on my hopes, dreams, and aspirations for the future. The dark voices would rise up in my head and say, "You don't deserve a great marriage and family. You've blown it, and you'll never find happiness again."

I kept my head up, and I refused to believe the lies. I chose to be tenacious.

2. Focus on a positive future.

By keeping your head up, you're able to see a positive future. If you're down on yourself and giving up on life, your head will hang low to the ground…satisfied with staring at all the things that have dropped away from your life.

If your eyes are lifted high and opened wide, you'll be able to see the incredible future that's in front of you. Yes, there are serious hurdles you're going to need to deal with, but you can do it…if your head is up. If your head is down (dark and depressed), you'll end up running into more obstacles. You won't even be able to see them coming!

Refuse to listen to the lies, and keep your head up toward the great future that awaits you.

3. Faith that Wisdom will guide you.

Part of keeping my head up means that I'm putting my faith into action…literally 'faithing.' I'm not sure where you are at in terms of faith or belief in a Higher Power, but holding my head up symbolizes a recognition of the One who is bigger than me.

If I personally believe that God created me and holds all Wisdom, I want to put my faith in God who also holds my future. Faithing looks like believing that your Creator has a plan and purpose for your path. Faithing means that I trust God to help me find beauty in the midst of the brokenness.

4. Trust your feelings to follow.

Oftentimes, I don't feel like holding my head up. In my darkest hours, I felt like crawling in a hole, curling up, and dying. Have you been there? Perhaps you're there right now?

I understand. I've felt all those dark feelings that make you want to quit trusting humanity, believing in a Higher Power, and just resign from this Earth. I've also felt the slow turning of my feelings toward hope. If I wait for that feeling before I take intentional action, it seems like the feelings take forever to show up.

Yet, if I hold my head high, and I start taking the actions I know to be true...those hope-filled feelings seem to start developing within me. They're like the caboose of my life...back there somewhere...slowly bring up the rear.

Keeping Your Shoulders Back

While you're in the process of lifting your head, why don't you go ahead and pull those shoulders back a bit as well? There's something equally as powerful about reminding yourself of the Strength that is at work within you. If you don't, slumped shoulders will produce a slumped life.

It's the strong foundation of your identity (who you are) that will allow you to take on a posture of power during this transitional season of life.

One of the challenges of keeping your shoulders back during or after a rough experience is that people will question your intentions. If you've been through a bankruptcy, some will wonder about your degree of responsibility. If you're walking through a divorce, others may ask if you're in denial. If you've just lost your job, your family may wonder why you're so upbeat.

Or, in my case, if you've caused great harm to your family, people may start attacking you to somehow make you 'pay' for your actions and make themselves feel better in the process. All the while, I held my head up...and I kept my shoulders back. As I read negative blog posts about my life and received countless emails from people who thought they knew what I needed to do next, I chose not to respond to these opinions.

In your case, you will have co-workers, classmates, former spouses, and anyone else who thinks they are wise come out of the woodwork to tell you what you need to do with your life. They'll see you in the midst of a challenging experience, and they'll know just what's right for you. You've probably already experienced it...unsolicited advice, passive-aggressive suggestions, outright criticism, and maybe even venomous attacks.

By keeping your shoulders back, you can...

1. **Choose to let others have their own opinions.**
   You can honor the 'right' we have as human beings to have a personal perspective on anything and everything. On top of that, someone has the power to share that opinion if they choose.

   I can honor and respect this right...but I don't have to 'value' what you say. To care about something means that I place value on your words, and I choose not to value everything that someone shares with me. You don't have to either.

2. **Value the opinions of those who walk closely with you.**
   As I was re-launching my life, there were three guys and a therapist who I relied upon strongly. Their thoughts and opinions about life and my situation were of the utmost importance to me. They were walking closely with me, and they knew my situation intimately. I could trust them.

   My wife's thoughts about my life are critical as well. We now have a partnership that relies upon open communication about everything – parenting, finances, spirituality, household duties, and time management. We are in a constant dialogue about our perspectives and opinions, and I value every thought and word that she shares with me.

   There are also a number of people who Laura and I have chosen to walk closely with in this life, and their perspective deeply matters to us. I don't necessarily play into their opinions...seeking their approval somehow. Instead, I ask them for input, and I listen. I care about what these individuals share...both affirming and challenging my life.

3. Listen to the opinions of those who experience you.
There are hundreds of people who experience you (through face-to-face interactions, workplace, school, social media, etc.), but they don't *really* know you. They can't know you. Although they may have an interaction with you, they are simply experiencing a part of who you are. When they share their thoughts or opinions about your life or situation, you don't have to place value on what they say.

In the process of listening to discern if I should 'value' their opinion, I take into account the health of their own life, their relational skills, any ulterior motives, their love for me, and their commitment to my best interests. It's amazing how often someone feels the need to share their unsolicited opinions, because they have a deep wound, fear, anxiety, or need to control the outcome of a situation. Oftentimes, a hint of truth is mixed in with a load of pain.

4. Disregard those who don't have your best interest in mind.
There are individuals who don't have your best interest in mind because of their own disappointment, lack of forgiveness, or self-righteousness. They want you to 'pay' for something. Unsolicited advice and opinions are generally weak in making an impact on your life. They go from person to person to thwart your positive actions in this world.

In general, people who are taking inventory of your life are simply trying to tear you down to lift themselves up. Our tendency is to point out the issues of another person when we have quite a few issues to deal with ourselves.

5. Humbly hold your own thoughts and perspectives.
Of course, you think you have the 'right' opinions, don't you? If you didn't, my guess is that you would change your opinion to

whatever you thought was best. The question is how firmly do you hold your opinions and how vocally do you express them?

For me, it just depends on the circumstances and the topic at hand. The process of humbly holding my opinions means that I recognize that I'm a flawed human being with only one perspective. Learning from the perspectives of others is absolutely key in order to see my own blind spots. Therefore, I welcome input…especially from those who I'm walking with through this life.

Taking One Step Forward
Head up…choosing a positive attitude about the future. Shoulders back…standing firm about the powerful foundation of who you are. And, take one step forward into the new normal you are creating!

One step forward…*one day at a time.*

I tend to run 100 miles per hour, but I really just need to be focused on the next step that's in front of me. If I take it one step at a time, I'll be able to focus on the things that matter most in my life. I won't get in a rush to get there faster than someone (or everyone) else. I won't be worried about seeing my entire life change within a few weeks or getting the life I've always wanted within a few months. It takes time, and all I need to be concerned about is the next step in front of me…today.

By asking the most important questions in my life, I'm able to take my next step each day…

> **Who am I?**
> Every step of the way, I need to remind myself of my identity… my divine imprint, strengths, wiring, and my story. This is the firm foundation that allows me to launch into the new future that's available to me.
>
> **What do I want?**
> Although there are so many things that people will offer me, I must remember what I truly want. What type of life is truly worth

living? I have been given one life...how will I invest it?

What truths will keep me focused?
As I'm re-launching my life, dark voices will rise up to dissuade me from taking one step forward today. They will try to convince me that going backward or sideways is best. I will not listen, and I will choose to focus on the truth.

How will I take action?
Knowing who I am and having a vision for my life is not enough. I must physically take action to experience the life I've always wanted. Do I know what I need to be doing today? Am I willing to courageously take that bold step?

Who will walk with me?
I realize that re-launching my life isn't something to be done alone. I must seek out the assistance of others and invite them to walk with me. There are many things I can learn from others, and more than anything, I simply need encouragement and support... and so do you.

As you ask these five questions over and over again in each of The Seven Spheres of Transformation, you'll begin to experience an empowerment to re-launch your entire life. You won't see all the results all at once, nor will you live life perfectly. Instead, you'll start to see the trajectory of your life change, and you'll begin to experience life in a brand new way.

In 2008, I was sick and tired of my life.

I made a decision that would lead me down a path of destruction as I searched for hope, peace, joy, and intimacy in this life. I hit rock bottom, and I wanted to give up. Thankfully, Hope intervened in my life, and I was given a second chance at a life launch.

I kept my head up, shoulders back, and started taking one step forward. I asked basic questions that seemed simple on the surface, but they ended up being more empowering than I could have ever imagined. I examined every facet of my life, and I questioned what I was doing and why. Slowly, I saw the transformation I longed for.

After being welcomed back home six months after leaving, I now have a partnership with my wife, Laura, that I had only hoped for in years past. We have a connected family environment where I love the time spent raising our children.

I'm no longer working 70-80 hours a week. Instead, I have my own marketing company where I set my own hours as I serve amazing clients. All the while, my wife and I are developing new friendships that are mutually encouraging, and we're part of a new church that's simple, organic, and life-giving. Before hitting rock bottom and re-launching, I didn't know this type of life was even possible.

I created a new normal, and so can you...
one intention at a time.

Also Available
by David Trotter

Lost + Found:
Finding Myself by Getting Lost in an Affair
After 10 years as a pastor, David was burned out and stuck in a life and marriage that lacked passion. His desire for an intimate partnership led him to leave his mistress of 'ministry' and run into the arms of a real-life mistress — his wife's best friend. After moving in with one another and spending forty days together, the woman abruptly left to go back to her husband and four kids, and David's life hit rock bottom.

This first-hand account of what led to his burnout and life implosion takes the reader on a raw and intimate journey…from illicit affair to hospitalization and ultimately to reconciliation with his wife and family. This is a powerful story of redemption that will leave the reader both challenged and inspired. (ISBN: 9781935798019)

AWAKEN my life
Through a raw, heartfelt essay and over 200 full color images captured along the back roads of rural India, "AWAKEN my life" calls out to hearts deadened by the continual pursuit of 'more.' Having bought into the promise of satisfaction which forever dangles like a carrot, hearts hunger and thirst for a rich and meaningful life. Perhaps your heart…

Are you open to see the world in a new way? Are you ready to be awakened? May you be awakened to the needs around the world (and even in your own neighborhood). May you allow the One who created you to set a new rhythm for your heart and your life. (ISBN: 9781935798002)

Acknowledgements
my appreciation

Laura
Thank you for being an incredible partner as we re-launched our lives, marriage, and family together. I love you, and I'm so thankful for a second chance to enjoy this life with you.

Waverly and Emerson
You are the most amazing kids in the entire world, and I'm so proud of you. Thank you for forgiving my poor decisions and loving me as your Daddy. You are so precious, and I'm so glad that God chose you for our family.

Mom and Dad
I deeply appreciate your ongoing support of me and my family. Your model of faithful love to one another in the midst of the ups and downs is inspiring and challenging. I love you both so much.

Randy Powell – www.journeyscounseling.com
Thank you for your undying support and encouragement. Your willingness to walk with me during my darkest days will never be forgotten. Your wisdom propelled me toward re-launching my life with both freedom and responsibility.

Suresh Kumar – www.harvestindia.org
You believe in me and the calling that God has placed upon my life. Thank you. You are a powerful coach and comrade who I'm so proud to be in relationship with. I love you.

Stacey Robbins – www.staceyrobbins.com
I deeply appreciate your input, challenge, and support. You are a cheerleader who I am honored to have in my corner. Your words of encouragement softly echo in my head when the dark voices start yelling loudly.

For more resources by David Trotter:
www.davidtrotter.tv

www.ingramcontent.com/pod-product-compliance
Lightning Source LLC
LaVergne TN
LVHW041332080426
835512LV00006B/421